The Gospel
and Unity

Institute for Ecumenical Research
Strasbourg, France

The Gospel Encounters History Series
Edited by Vilmos Vajta

In cooperation with: Günther Gassmann, Marc Lienhard, Harding Meyer, Warren A. Quanbeck, Michael Rogness, and Gérard Siegwalt.

The Gospel
and Unity

Edited by
Vilmos Vajta

Augsburg Publishing House
Minneapolis, Minnesota

THE GOSPEL AND UNITY

261·9
Gb94

184091

Contents

Preface

The present volume is the first of a series which carries the overall title *The Gospel Encounters History*. In these volumes on ecumenical subjects Lutheran scholars will call attention to the fact that in its task to interpret the gospel, theology is summoned to encounter its own history with the contemporary historical situation. The many appeals for renewal in church and theology call for such a response.

The introduction included in this volume is a joint attempt by the editorial board to outline the task of these volumes. Also the essays themselves are prepared in a consultation among the authors to harmonize the volume's basic orientation. Each author, however, is responsible for his own manuscript.

The publication of this series follows earlier volumes by Lutheran theologians concerning the issues raised by the Second Vatican Council: *(The Papal Council and the Gospel, Dialogue on the Way,* and *Challenge and Response,* published by Augsburg Publishing House, Minneapolis, Minnesota). In the light of recent ecumenical events — Church and Society Conference in Geneva, 1966; the World Council of Churches Assembly in Uppsala, 1968; and the Lutheran World Federation Assembly in Evian, 1970 — time now seemed opportune for a study on the wide scope of contemporary ecumenical discussion. Through these volumes we invite the reader to follow these critical reflections of present trends in ecumenical thinking.

Warren A. Quanbeck and Michael Rogness carried special responsibility for the English edition of this volume, with Ulrich Reetz acting as editorial assistant.

We express our deep gratitude to the Evangelical Lutheran Church of Bavaria, whose generous donation to the Lutheran Foundation for Ecumenical Research made this whole project possible. We also thank Augsburg Publishing House for cooperation in publishing this series.

Institute for Ecumenical Research
Strasbourg, France

Introduction:

RENEWAL IN THEOLOGY

THE SITUATION
The New History

God, the creator and preserver of the universe and of everything that lives and sustains life, calls a people from among the many peoples of the earth and makes them his people. Thus God's one history with his world takes on the quality of a "new history." God calls this people to an exodus out of bondage, idleness, self-satisfaction, and resignation. He makes a covenant with them and leads them into the path of new obedience. When they turn away from him, look back, and seek to make themselves comfortable in the status quo, he raises up in their midst prophets who call them to repentance. In addition, these prophets direct the people's gaze into the future in the expectation and promise of a new act of God in history for his people, for all mankind.

In Jesus Christ God's new history takes on universal dimensions.
The new history is testified to, described, and unfolded for all times by the manifold voices of his disciples, apostles, and followers. God makes this new history penetrate into and become incarnate in human history through the living word of proclamation, in the power of the sacraments, through the discipleship of the believers and through the reign of the living Christ over this world. In so far as his grace and the revelation of his will in Jesus Christ is and was

9

unknown and ineffective in this human history, it could be designated as "old history." In it Jesus Christ places all men before
the decision of repentance and new obedience in the world. His
cross passes judgment on the old self-righteous man and on every
fearful, self-assured, or irrational submission to the currently dominant standards, thought structures, and social orders of this world.
The cross reveals the temporary nature of human history and frees
man for a new kind of thought and action. Jesus' resurrection is
the victory over all the evil powers, the dethronement of all who
claim absolute authority, the overcoming of unrighteousness and
inhumanity, and the hope and conviction that all human life has
its goal in him. This new history will find its consummation at the
return of Jesus Christ. Its consummation is the consummation of
his reign. Until then, the new history is in flux and the church of
Jesus Christ, the new humanity of God's new history, testifies to
and embodies this movement between incarnation and parousia.
Therefore, the call to repentance from complacency and imprison-
ment in the past goes out ever anew to the wandering people of
God in changing times and different places. Trusting in the guidance of the Holy Spirit and considering their own future and the
world's future, the people of God must in every new time and situation ask, think through, proclaim, and do what the Lord commands
them through the voices of his witnesses.

Repeatedly in the history of the church, through changing situations, lines of confrontation, and challenges of their time, individual
Christians have realized anew the gift of God's new history with
his people. With good reason we designate such new breakthroughs
as "movements of renewal." In them, Christian thought and action
has attempted to become free from ties to the torpid systems of
their outmoded past. The gospel is heeded anew, God's judgment
and promise are proclaimed, and the call to repentance and to
renewal of the spirit is obeyed. In the modern age, the Reformation
of the 16th century, the rise of ecumenical movements in the 20th
century, and the Second Vatican Council are examples and road-
markers of these movements of renewal. Therefore, in a new
theological concern for the larger themes of gospel, history, man,
church, and church unity, they cannot and must not be ignored.

The Reformation churches, other churches, and increasingly

the Roman Catholic Church, are still determined by the Reformation's historical consequences and new theological point of departure. A personal, responsible struggle for the decision and understanding of faith took the place of an authoritarian religious-ecclesiastical system. But beyond that, the Reformation, with its rediscovery of the sovereign, redeeming grace of God in Jesus Christ, gave back to Christendom a basic expression of the gospel which remains fundamental for our present thought as a hermeneutical key for understanding the biblical message. At the same time, that fundamental expression of the gospel can and should keep us from understanding as absolute norms the theological consensus and the theologies of the Reformation and the churches which, in cooperation or in conflict with secular history, grow out of those theologies. The sovereign and redeeming grace of God, expressed anew 450 years ago, must be proclaimed in our time with new words and new signs of its realization.

With the ecumenical movement of the 20th century, a rediscovery of another aspect of God's new history has appeared. In this new history and in the new humanity, whose beginning is Jesus Christ and whose temporary embodiment his church is called to be, the boundaries between races, nations, cultures, classes, political and social systems, and now also between denominations and churches which were established in the old history are to be overcome. We are standing in the midst of this movement. Because it is a movement, it cannot come to a stop at a certain level in the development of its structures and its goals but rather must be driven further forward by new approaches, each of which must be critically examined. We cannot step out of that movement, unless we want to shut ourselves out of God's new history and its progress.

The Second Vatican Council took up and to a great extent acknowledged earlier scattered endeavors and a widespread longing for the renewal of the Roman Catholic church. Basic biblical statements were reconfirmed, the first steps toward a reform of the shape of the church were taken, and the way was prepared for an opening of the church toward the world. The council was the point of departure and the stimulant for an increasingly tension-ridden struggle in many parts of the Roman Catholic church for the renewal of theology and church; nonCatholic Christendom cannot follow in the attitude of an indifferent spectator. Roman Catholics and Christians of other denominations see themselves face to face with a world which, in its need, its divisions, its alienation, and its helplessness, awaits a new, credible proclamation and convincing signs of God's new history with his people and his world. The answers to these challenges from the world can be found and realized only through a joint, reciprocally stimulating and correcting seeking and striving for renewal.

God's new history demands a continuous renewal of the church, and it works its way deep into the history of this world, seeking to change it. Therefore, all renewal of theology and church must pay heed to the voices, structures, and variety of this world, which is God's creation and the sphere of Jesus Christ's reign, in a responsible participation in its future. But this inquiry and participation are something different than a falsely understood *aggiornamento* in the sense of an uncritical accommodation to the expectations and answers of our time and world. Until the consummation of his reign, the cross and resurrection of Jesus Christ will remain promise *and* judgment for the world.

Therefore, theology and church will always have to take up the task of the creative nonconformist. Over against every self-assured optimism about progress they must call to mind the temporal nature, the limitations and perils of human existence and history. Only then can they contribute to a realistic view and formation of the present and future. Only in this way can they be tools and signs of the power of God's new history at work transforming human history.

The Challenge from the World

God's new history, beginning with the call of the people of Israel and entering into a more comprehensive dimension with Jesus Christ, was the liberation of men from the deadening religious and secular orders of the time, a liberation of repentance and renewal. Called to be the new community of the redeemed, the church *has betrayed this new history again and again* by accommodating itself without reservation to the currently dominant powers in the intellectual and social spheres. It has become their servant or even their master and has concealed the gospel's life-giving power and God's free grace under an all-inclusive religious system of rules and regulations. Just as human history shows evidence of the transforming effects of God's new history, so likewise the history of the church and theology is blurred by the old history of men, which was overcome in Christ. This ambivalence and this struggle will continue until all is united in Jesus Christ in the consummated reign of God.

Therefore certain modern developments in the history of ideas and society are also understood as the consequences of this disavowal of God's new history by the church and theology. Is not the postChristian *atheism* also a radical rejection of a theological concept of God in which the hidden and revealed reality of God beyond our own ideas of God was lost? Is it not a rejection of a working hypothesis of "God" which the churches called upon all too quickly for help with those troublesome questions which they could not answer? Is not the modern *secularization* also an act of liberation from a religious system of total world control, which was really constructed as a "work of man"? Are not the *revolutionary movements* of our time, which want to liberate man from the constant threat to his existence and the contempt for his dignity in need, dependence, alienation, segregation, and manipulation and to lead him to his true manhood, also an answer to the inability or unwillingness of Christians to let the transforming power of the new humanity and God's new history be effective in the structures of this world?

These movements too, then, are a call to repentance and renewal for theology and the church today. Only the answer to them must find its point of departure not in these movements themselves, but rather in the biblical testimony of God's new history. To answer modern atheism with a "post-God-is-dead-theology" is to fall back into the disavowal of theology, so vehemently criticized today, in favor of a conformity to the currently dominant intellectual trends. But the answer also cannot consist of referring to a being which reposes in transcendence or to a power or a relationship which is encompassed within immanence. We must proclaim the Lord who stands above the world and history as the one who is at work in the midst of this world and history in a hidden yet self-revealing way. The theological affirmation of secularization as the liberation of the world from the tutelage of religion must be tied to the proclamation of the reign of Jesus Christ over God's creation and to the execution of the church's mission to the world. That affirmation will have to respect the "No" to faith as a human alternative. But it will have to apply itself critically against tendencies in secularism which place the world's autonomy in place of God and deny the dialectic of the world, which consists of the world's being accepted by God and its enmity against God. Above all, it will resolutely unmask new, absolute, and quasi-religious value standards.

And finally, theology and church will support with all their power the concerns for the *humanum,* which have become so central in our time. But in so doing they must challenge the idea of the self-sufficient man, who is lifted up as the standard of man and who then usurps for himself, as a substitute God, unlimited political, scientific, or technological power over other men. In addition, the church will have to proclaim and live the fact that man's true *humanum* is first realized in his communion with God and in the subsequent new, fraternal, just, and free communion of men in their common bond to the will of God as it is revealed in Jesus Christ.

Thus the movements named here as characteristic for our present day are connected with God's new history in a threefold manner: (1) they are consequences of the fall of theology and church back into the structures and behavior patterns of the old history, which is not yet fully penetrated by the new history; (2) they force the Christian in his thought and action to self-examination, and summon him to the repentance and renewal which is necessary; (3) they are the object of Christian affirmation and solidarity, but which includes a simultaneous critical exposure and rejection of those elements which stem from the old history.

The New Humanity in the Old World and History

The church of Jesus Christ is the point of intersection of God's history with the world and human history. From what has been

said until now it is clear that this cannot mean a point of intersection between a vertical line and a horizontal line or between
two lines running towards each other. The lines which intersect
in the church are not simply the lines of the pure, unveiled, and
powerful proclamation and embodiment of the gospel of Christ,
and of the world, alienated from God and abandoned to its secularity. God's new history, which manifests itself in the new humanity — begun in Jesus Christ and continued in the church — is
a history of salvation which is hidden under the encroachments of
the old history and which only seldom breaks through to unambiguous clarity. Error, blindness, and sin are abolished in Christ.
Nevertheless, in the history of the church and in the history of
the individual Christian they are fellow-travelers with the new
humanity which have not yet been driven out for good.

But another movement, in the opposite direction, now also takes
its place along side of this influence of the old history on the
church. While the old world and history, in their alienation from
God and enmity against God, stand opposite the church and
influence it, on the other hand they are already being penetrated
and transformed by the powers of God's new history. For they are
God's creation and the area in which Christ's reign is at work;
they are the locus of Christian existence and bear the traces of
the new history's world-transforming power, which is introduced
into them through the proclamation and the service of Christians.
Thus in the church, the line of God's new history, though veiled
by elements of the old history and world, intersects with the line
of the world's old history, which has now been taken into the
process of the advance of the new history. Hence the church's
ambiguous, dialectic, and tension-filled nature, which clearly can
be reduced neither to a mere church-world relationship nor to the
previously drawn differentiations of divine-human, visible-invisible,
or hidden-manifest.

But if we must adhere to the assertion that the church, so
interwoven with the old and the new history, has its ever re-creating
basis in proclamation, sacrament, and mission, through which God's
new history is imparted to it and through which it is introduced
into this new history, then the church's situation is at all times
determined by the *tension between temptation and promise.* Temp-

tation, because it may want to replace or repress the gift and the task of the new history in favor of the very much easier and often more triumphant way of accommodation to the given realities and expectations of the old world. Promise, because in obedience to its Lord and through repentance and renewal it paves the way for the force of God's new history to work. Thus the church can let its thought and action be liberated from the clutches of the old history. On this road of renewal the church itself, following its Lord and accepting the judging and liberating power of his cross and resurrection, can again become a trail blazer of God's new history in the world.

Theology has the special task of being the conscience of the church. In self-critical examination, theology must ask itself whether it has not all too often provided the church with the legitimation of its lapse into the old history. Theology must ask itself whether, through its restriction to the academic sphere, it has not abandoned the church in its helplessness in the face of the powers of the old and the new struggling within it. Over against this failure in its real task, theology must at every time and in every situation strive for *repentance and for the renewal of its thought*. Only in this way can it serve the church of Jesus Christ by probing, clarifying, and proclaiming the biblical testimony of the liberating and creative power of the Christ's gospel in the context of the intellectual and social movements of our time. Theology has its sole *raison d'être* in this service to the present and future course of the church, which constantly needs renewal.

THE TASK
The Task in View of the Present Reality

We understand and describe *reality* today not so much in the categories of nature but rather much more as *history*. In this way we are able to keep in mind the nature of the world's past, present, and future as something which is temporary, ambivalent, fluctuating, and challenging. Moreover, we say that in the view of the Christian faith this reality is determined by man's old history and God's new history with his humanity. Both bear the features of the historical: they are in flux and they challenge us. If they must

also be differentiated theologically, clearly they cannot, as a historical reality, be separated and set in opposition to each other as
salvation history and secular history, or as history of salvation and
history of judgment. In both, with their point of intersection in the
church, the powers of the other are effective — as renewal or as
apostasy, as temptation or as promise. God, the creator and preserver, is Lord over both.

This perpetually active God is no metaphysical being which
reposes in himself. In his revelation through Jesus Christ and in his
new covenant with men, he shows himself to be the living Lord of
all reality who drives his new history forward and transforms the
old history through it. The historical dimension of reality and of
God's action is marked by *personal relationships*. The reality of
the world is no longer understood as a product of superhuman
natural powers, but rather as the place where men rule. The man
of the old and of the new covenant, the new humanity, is called
to be the image of and fellow-worker with God. He stands under
the judgment, the redeeming grace, the demand, and the promise
of God in Jesus Christ. In this response of obedience God's new
history becomes incarnate and concrete in conjunction and conflict
with the old history of men. In this personal confrontation with
the God who reveals himself in Jesus Christ as "God with us,"
man receives his true manhood as one called to be responsible in
listening and in responding. This personal relationship comes
about only in the context of the Word, sacrament, and mission,
elements which establish the church. Therefore, in community with
the forerunners and brothers in the faith and in the social structures
of the world, this relationship must not be understood in a narrow
actualistic or individualistic sense. This dialog of God with man
must also find its "extension" within a dialog in which a theology
struggling for renewal unites with theologians, theologies, and
beliefs beyond the boundaries of its own church, its own discipline,
even its own beliefs, in the search for the truth.

In the face of the present tremendous scientific and technological
progress, through which the reality of nature, man, and history is
being illuminated and increasingly mastered, there no longer appears to be any place for the dimension of the *mysterious*. But if
reality is also understood as the sphere of God's reign, it then

becomes clear that reality does possess this dimension of the mysterious. Only in realizing this is a comprehensive understanding of reality possible. God's activity in history and through men is demonstrable only seldom — we can only try to point to its traces in retrospect. God in his activity is always ahead of us. He revealed himself in Jesus Christ in the veil of human form, suffering and dying on the cross. Likewise he reveals himself today in the weak and fallible word of men, he is still the hidden God who appears to be infinitely distant from us and yet perhaps is right next to us, driving his new history forward in the yearning and struggling of men or groups.

A renewal in theology can take place only by recognizing and taking seriously the historical, personal, and hidden dimension of reality and of the ruling activity of God.

The Sources

Today, the renewal of theology finds its basis, authority, and orientation in the *biblical testimony* to God's new history. As the word of men the biblical writings reflect the revelation of God's new history in Jesus Christ in many diverse ways. They are not the revelation itself, but rather can always only become revelation, in the power of the Holy Spirit; when and where God wills. Since the biblical testimony is manifold and contingent upon men, it should be indisputable that critical biblical research is necessary; but it should also be equally indisputable that the goal of this research is to work out with the greatest possible clarity the basic lines of the new history, continuously testified to and confessed by the entire Scripture, and to open up ways to understand them. The lasting authority of the Bible's human testimony, verified ever anew and brought repeatedly to new effectiveness by the Holy Spirit, rests on the fact that it — together with its earlier forms as oral traditions — stands in unequaled proximity to the original revelation-event and has its origin in the disciples, apostles, and followers commissioned and empowered by the earthly and the resurrected Jesus Christ. Despite the contingent nature and all the differences of these witnesses and this testimony, we can here read God's new history most clearly. God's ongoing activity in history is hidden under the ambiguity of the interweaving of the old and new history, and we must venture to probe it only under the direction of and with the criterion of the original testimony and with a forward-looking trust in the guidance of the Holy Spirit.

In the changing situations, dangers, and challenges in the church's history, the Scripture's original testimony or individual aspects of it had to be reconfirmed and unfolded anew for the current situation. The handing down, the "tradition," of the biblical testimony, which in turn was the depositing of a tradition, is actualized in *the church's confession;* this confession is expressed spontaneously here and there, in past and present, but at crucial points in church history it takes on binding form as a formal confession of the universal faith. These confessions are subject to the norm of Holy Scripture, and the ecclesiastical and theological traditions which grow out of them must be confronted in every age with the critical question whether they hinder or help the advance of God's new history. The traditional confessions are significant roadmarks on the path of God's new history through the old history. They cannot be ignored by a theology which is struggling for renewal and which is conscious of its own history and historicity; likewise they also cannot replace the on the spot confession of the moment, which actualizes and concretizes the original testimony in a new time and situation in prayer, praise, testimony, teaching, and service.

The Holy Scripture and the church's confession are anchored in the *worship service,* which serves God's new history by gathering the congregation together and sending it forth. The congregation's confession before God and in the world constantly receives new impulses from the interpretative proclamation, the testimony, and the teaching of Holy Scripture. Vice versa, new possibilities for understanding Scripture are opened by this confession and witness which occurs in the context of the world's needs, questions, and challenges, all of which are echoed in the congregation's worship service. Emphasizing and preserving this inter-relationship guards us from an intellectualization of faith and especially from a biblical and denominational fundamentalism — which often arises simultaneously. This fundamentalism ignores God's new history, because it is not ready to admit that history itself, and thereby also the understanding, attestation, and verification of it, is in flux.

But it is not only Scripture and confession which are anchored in worship. The interrelationship between *leitourgia,* worship of God, and *diakonia,* ministry to men, is also expressed in it. The praising and thanking celebration of God's new history and the more comprehensive fulfilment of worship as service to God in the form of one's neighbor have belonged to the life of the church from its very beginning. If one of these two aspects of worship is neglected or suppressed, then the other aspect is no longer true and sincere worship of God. Renewal in theology is only possible when theology is nourished by the celebration and the occurrence of God's new history in worship's interrelationship of Scripture and confession, *leitourgia* and *diakonia,* and when theology itself contributes to a renewal of the understanding and forms of this all-inclusive worship of God.

Knowledge

The new history is *God's* history and can, because it is interwoven with all reality, be understood only historically. Therefore, all theological knowledge must be viewed and must take place within the structure of *fullness and progress.* In the revelation of God in Jesus Christ, this new history and thereby God as its creator and Lord, Jesus Christ as its lasting realization, and the Holy Spirit as its driving power, have entered into the old world and history in their fullness and entirety. The new history in its fullness and entirety is a gift from God. As such it makes possible our relationship to God and our true manhood. It also makes our theological knowledge possible, though the new history is not something which is mastered by theological knowledge. It can never be known fully and with ultimate clarity, because it presents itself to us only in a historically conditioned form and tradition, and yet nevertheless in that form and tradition it addresses us and appeals to us as ultimate reality. The task of theological knowledge is to probe this fullness ever anew and to express it, striving for the greatest possible approximation to its truth, as a service to the church and to its proclamation and action. In doing this it sometimes takes the wrong road and neglects its task, but at the same time it is given new insights, so that we can speak — with Scripture — of a growing in knowledge and truth. In this growth we can neither transcend the temporary nature of dogmatic statements nor ever capture the fullness of the mystery of revelation. Renewal in theology takes place by knowing that God has given the ability to know and the ability to overcome the temporary nature of previous knowledge through an advancing struggle — which consciously assumes a new temporal nature — for the truth of God's new history.

This constant struggle to know, proclaim, and accept the truth has a greater potential for growth and deepening when it takes place in the form of the *ecumenical dialog.* In the consideration, clarification, acceptance, and modification of the gracious gifts of knowledge given to the church of Jesus Christ, there develops process of seeking the truth which can point to that fullness of the mystery of revelation being realized in God's new history in a more comprehensive manner than is possible for an individually or denominationally limited theological endeavor. At the same time, the dialog form of theological knowledge of the truth also offers the chance to proceed beyond a merely tactical, superficially tolerant, or resigned acceptance of theological variety to an affirmation of differing terminologies, thought-forms, and contents as the components of a seeking theological existence, as a constructive expression of the inexhaustible fullness of the divine truth, and as a sign of the lasting limited and temporary nature of theological striving for knowledge. The currently pressing and still unsolved problem of a demarcation of a legitimate variety over against church-dividing opposites can be solved only through a joint theological undertaking, with a view to the new points now held in common, plus new differences and lines of conflict now penetrating all churches in like manner. In so far as the ecumenical dialog overcomes the church-dividing past and present, theology is liberated from its fixation to old controversies and denominational self-justifications which, in the process of the dialog, prove to be outmoded. Thus in the reciprocally stimulating ecumenical dialog, theology gains new room and new energies to work towards its renewal, with a view to the forward looking witness and activity of the whole church of Jesus Christ in God's new history.

The following statement could possibly be put forward as a
theological tenet: full *authority* for our thought and action belongs
only to the fullness of God's new history revealed in Jesus Christ
while theological striving for knowledge about this history must
only and always lead to the *crisis* of every theological undertaking.
Such a statement leads us into the heart of the problem. Precisely
because God's new history became incarnate in human history
and thus became accessible to human knowledge, it confronts our
ability to know not in its pure divine fullness and clarity, but
rather always in its reflection and effects in history. Just as the
new history and the old history are interwoven in each other, so
also for us there can be no clear division between the authority
and the crisis of theological knowledge. From this it results that
theological knowledge and statements have authority since they,
in the context of their own time and situation, open themselves to
the fullness of the divine revelation and, trusting in the Holy Spirit,
are able to know and express it anew. A necessary element of this
openness is knowing the impossibility and the presumptuousness
of the attempt to claim or even to secure institutionally for one's
own perception of the truth (which is historically conditioned,
stands under the eschatological reservation and is therefore temporary and in need of deepening and revision) that authority which
belongs only to the divine fullness. The criterion of this relative
authority, which is never totally free from uncertainty, can only
be the original testimony of Holy Scripture, which, even though it
itself is historically conditioned, nevertheless expresses the fullness
of God's new history more comprehensively than all others. To
that can be added such interpretations and attestations of this
criterion in the confessions and in the growing knowledge of the
church and of theology as have proven up to now historically
effective in their approximation to the fullness and therefore in
their relative authority. Thus authority can never be asserted or
demanded as a rightful claim; that would be to fail to recognize
the locus of theology as a striving for knowledge which is constantly in flux and which starts out from hearing and receiving.
Authority lies only in the claim on us of God's liberating visitation
and declaration of his will in and through Jesus Christ, as well as
in the deep experience of theological knowledge, effected by the

Holy Spirit and contained in this new history. This can only happen when theology constantly strives for its own renewal so it can thus serve God's new history. This renewal is only possible when theology knows it is bound to the biblical witness, takes seriously the confession of the church, and is oriented to the worship of the new humanity in *leitourgia* and *diakonia*. It must meet the needs, passions, and challenges of the world in willingness to question, to be questioned, to respond and to serve the renewal and mission of the church. It must be conscious of the temporary and partial nature and therefore of the necessary growth of all knowledge of the truth.

GÜNTHER GASSMANN

MARC LIENHARD

HARDING MEYER

WARREN A. QUANBECK

MICHAEL ROGNESS

GÉRARD SIEGWALT

VILMOS VAJTA

Chapter I

Theology in Dialog

When we talk about a renewal of theology, we must seriously consider the importance of dialog as a theological method. Such a consideration, in turn, highlights two theological tendencies of the present time — a theology of the ecumenical dimension, which is the endeavor of the various Christian bodies engaged in dialog with each other in the ecumenical movement, and a theology of the secular dimension, which emphasizes the ties of the Christian faith to all mankind. A theological study which bases its research on these two spheres of relationship must of necessity concern itself with the method of dialog.[1] In the following, the importance of this new field of inquiry for the study of theology in the ecumenical movement is to be spelled out. In particular, attention is drawn to the contribution which, in its role as a critic, this method can make towards the understanding of theological insights. Here, no more than an outline can be attempted. It will require a more detailed and thorough treatment at some future date.

THE THEOLOGY OF A CHURCH IN DIALOG

The demand for a theology of dialog might, at first sight, appear to be pandering to the spirit of our age. If it were, it would be easy to dismiss the challenge by pointing to the need for theology to retain its independent character. However, the peculiar nature of theological study surely stems from the particular subject matter, which forms the basis for any theological research. Our first task, then, would be to find out whether or not this subject matter of theology admits to dialog as part of its nature. If we succeed in producing positive evidence along this line, we shall not have to face an element foreign to theology, but one which, in its own right, would enrich theology. It might even be the means of bettering and deepening people's understanding of what theology has to say about God in our age. That is the aim of this essay. As our starting point, we shall have to take certain hypotheses which have been worked out elsewhere and will be mentioned here in outline only.[2]

Dialog complies with the nature of the *ecclesia* as the *koinonia* of the Holy Spirit. It gives and receives part of that reality which is God's gift. This mutual giving and receiving has within it the essential life of communion with God. Yet, in this context, it can also be seen, as a communion through dialog, as the life of an essential relationship, which has its source in the covenant relationship of God with mankind. In this relationship with God, the element of dialog unfolds itself in the process of the edifying of the body of Christ by means of a living exchange of the gifts of the Spirit in the members of the body. This gives the concept of dialog a deeper meaning, which lies beyond the structure of thinking, in the sphere of human existence itself.

This new ecclesiological vision today revives the original intentions of the doctrine of the priesthood of all believers (which was later interpreted individualistically) by means of new ideas, e.g., that of participation or of collegiality. This should, of necessity, have its effect on the work of theology. In an *ecclesia* structured on dialog, only a theology of dialog can be true to its own essential nature. At this point, however, two forms of monolog in theology are brought into question simultaneously: on the one hand, that of proclaiming Christian truth in monolog, looking on it as an unalterable deposit; on the other hand, that of specific research by means of monolog, without any existential communication with or by the *ecclesia*. This questioning of the monolog goes further than merely its technicalities. It touches on its essence. Having said this, it must be admitted that, at times, you can have a dialog in spite of the absence of a formal conversation between different partners. After all, even when viewed as a structure of human thought, dialog is more than a two-way conversation in the accepted sense of the word, since it could still be no more than a process of verbally bypassing each other. For dialog should demand from each partner the endeavor to put himself into the place of the other as far as his thought structure is concerned. This, however, involves us in important existential decisions, which tend to lie beyond the technique of talking with the other person.

Dialog is determined by existential communication, addressing itself to the very being of man. It is bound to result in anthropological insights which are vital also for theology. Even against this theological background, dialog is to be seen in a new light. In this way, theological consciousness affects the concept of dialog: instead of being adopted as something second-hand, dialog has, in its own right, a vital say in theological matters. In other words, theology has an intrinsic call to develop the nature of dialog. On the grounds of its insights, it claims the right of contributing to the dialog between the sciences by making pronouncements on the existential communication of man. Understood in this way, the claims of the theology of dialog are the claims of theology itself. It will, therefore, be necessary to make a critical assessment of the concept of dialog in the present situation, before we can achieve genuine theological self-determination for the theology of dialog.

DIALOG AND THEOLOGY

First, we shall try to show the link between the concrete phenomenon of dialog and the task of theology.

Types of Dialog

Pluralism and Dialog. Life in modern society, including the spiritual sector, offers us a great variety of social, political, ideological, and religious convictions. The monolithic culture of the past has disintegrated. Worldwide communications of mankind today mean that every one of us is faced not only with different culture but also with different world views. We therefore speak of a pluralistic society, which has replaced the old monolithic order. It is into a situation like this that dialog enters as a vital form of man's social behavior. It offers a modern variant of what tolerance was in former epochs, in which man, much as he might have wanted to, was unable to arrest the advance of a monolithic culture. He lacked the necessary means of power — or, where these were still available, they were overruled by primary interests — to replace the variety of views by a single, privileged order. He tolerated the others without thereby acknowledging their right to exist. The same applies today with regard to the multiple forms of dialog. In our pluralistic society, it means virtually no more than patient tolerance towards people of other convictions by the sheer force of circumstance in a given situation. The alternative would be worldwide apartheid, but few find this acceptable. "Friendly coexistence" has become one of the most powerful modern slogans. Yet, in the first place, it shows no more than resignation of will in the face of unconditional equation with the others. At the same time, it is the tentative resignation vis-á-vis any (including the theological brand of) "dogmatism." For such resignation does not contain respect for the others, but only the recognition of one's inability to assert his own position.

Dialog also finds its advocates among those who suffer from intellectual resignation in the form of skepticism. The emergence of a pluralistic society has revived this as a relevant attitude. Where many things are tolerated, many things can be true. And where anything can be true, practically nothing is true. A skeptic is consequential in advocating dialog if he does not expect anything from it beyond the simple knowledge of the existence of the other, intrinsically uninteresting though the other may be. In this context, dialog becomes an intellectual game. The victory of doubting truth itself is celebrated in noncommittal conversation. When everything is subjected to dialog by way of a kind of "pandialogism," search after truth in the real sense of dialog is out of the question. Talking to one another in this way can hardly be described as dialog.

Involvement and Dialog. Opponents of dialog never tire of arguing that it neutralizes the problem of truth and, by admitting a multiplicity of different attitudes, altogether renounces faith in the one truth. Justified as this criticism may be with regard to the (improper) forms of dialog mentioned above, it certainly does not apply to that deeper perception which touches the essential nature of dialog. For here, the different attitudes are involved in an encounter marked by the problem of truth, and witness to the one truth by searching for it in togetherness.

Pluralism by no means implies an indiscriminate and chaotic multiplicity, nor does it mean indifference towards the various attitudes. Rather, it can be instrumental in bringing about a confrontation, not by preventing a clash of different attitudes, but by helping truth to vindicate itself in the conflict of views. Clearly, it is not the function of dialog to uphold one of the given views and to lend it final validity. On the contrary, commitment to truth may lead to the discovery of the ingredients of truth in the various pronouncements without even the attempt of a synthesis. The same truth can be recognized from a variety of viewpoints. Different ways of thinking can provide it with a framework, without necessarily having to lose their own identities, provided that there is no doubt about the coherence of the one truth and that nobody presupposes the plurality of truth itself. For within the various concrete "truths" of the pronouncements and the different situations, there still operates the same reality of truth which is known and affirmed by attitudes held in plurality.[3] Pluralistic society has taught man that he can no longer think by himself. The transition from the thinking of man to the thinking of mankind has taken place,[4] and this has made it possible to call for dialog as an indispensable catalyst in this process. The teamwork in many fields of science provides ample evidence for this.

The results which mankind has achieved through this thinking in dialog far outreach anything that could have been achieved in individual isolation. It is unlikely that such thinking as is controlled by dialog might lead to a pluralistic diversification through a multiplicity of truths. Rather, it serves the one truth in its diversity. In fact, dialog helps us in our pluralistic society to secure the full value of this plurality as a treasure belonging to the whole of mankind, to cultivate it and to bring it to fruition. The thinking of mankind in togetherness does not absolve man from being a genuine person — it helps him to give full expression to his being.[5] For it is in the concrete relationship to somebody else, in my consciousness of the dependency of my own being on that of the other person, that my personal life comes fully into flower. The "I" arises from the "thou" of the other person and irresistibly draws me into the great fellowship of dialog within mankind. At this point, there arises an involvement with dialog which, in its essence, is prompted by the evolvement of one's own personal life as a part of the whole.[6] Its structure is different from that of the whole. Mankind, involved in a meaningful dialog within itself, is looking ahead, bent on the future and therefore full of hope. In its search for truth, it witnesses to the goal in which it believes and to which it addresses all its energies, enriched by its diversity.

In our demand for a theology of dialog, we should be careful to distinguish between these two forms of dialog. In a pluralistic society, it should help us to clarify our spiritual thinking if we point out that, in the face of a pluralism which is indifferent to the truth, the essential dialog of mankind can say yes to a plurality of attitudes precisely because it reflects man's search for truth and continually leads to new discoveries of it.

A theology of dialog will, in the nature of things, adhere to this latter form of dialog, because in it, as will later be shown in greater detail, it is given a vision of how it can attain to the full evolution of its own peculiar being in complete freedom.

The Ecumenical Dialog

When you look at the ecumenical movement in our century and ask yourself what is the role that dialog plays within it, you will not find it easy to give a clear answer. There are, within the movement, several strata of understanding of what is meant by ecumenical commitment to a reconciling theological dialog. These different strata are still shifting their positions, since it has been only during the last few years that the nature of dialog has been emphasized. In all this, it is difficult to decide whether it is the "proper" kind of dialog that is under discussion, or simply a new version of the noncommittal type of conversation. We cannot do more than delineate some of the chief tendencies, bearing in mind that even if one or the other tendency occasionally predominates, they never appear as separate entities, either in time or on principle.

First of all, the ecumenical movement offers the opportunity of *becoming acquainted with* the different church traditions and theological positions. Initially, "they" are little more than objects under examination, and the interest involved is confessionally orientated. While endeavoring a high degree of objectivity in gathering the information, we are, as yet, not prepared for a genuine encounter. We are first concerned with the demarcation of the boundaries so we can distinguish between our own position and that of the others. However helpful such a knowledge of the theological positions may be, it can hardly be described as dialog. This has already been pointed out.[7] For this method has merely been able to relate the findings of ecumenical conferences by way of stating what "some thought," what "others thought" and what "others again thought." This method fulfills the purpose of demarcating positions, but that is as far as it can go.

This is also true of the method of dialectics which, under the influence of Karl Barth, marked the reports of Amsterdam 1948 and only succeeded in highlighting the fact that the structure of it all was far too complicated. They spoke of "Unity in Disunity" or of "Disunity in Unity." [8] As far as method is concerned, this did not help them to advance towards dialog with each other. Their own positions were still unalterably fixed.

Although it was soon discovered that, as far as the denominations were concerned, the boundaries could not be determined by ecclesiastical law, a real encounter of the different schools of thought was not achieved. One met the others in order to give information about oneself, possibly even in order to teach them or to convert them to the truth. Not only professional statements but also expert papers by theologians have been known to use this method in ecumenical conferences.

At the same time, however, an atmosphere of *trust* developed. The straightforward human encounter, the experience of the witness and the courage of conviction on the part of those others, who also confessed the name of Jesus, brought about a certain liking for them. Even though you could not share their theological position, you could at least appreciate it. Furthermore, by actively caring for people in their spiritual and bodily needs, a common ground was discovered and a challenge that could be met together

by people even of different church traditions and theological schools
of thought. It was not long before the demand "to do together
whatever could be done together" found willing ears and led to a
situation in which many went their separate ways only where the
particular religious experience of the one or the other made this
inevitable. It also became possible with mutual trust to work on
common texts. Often this made it necessary to reach only minimal
agreement, and as a result, much of this was looked upon as com-
promise, i.e., as an attempt to meet each other halfway by refrain-
ing from saying everything that, on one's own part, was felt to be
true. Thus it was regard for the others — not necessarily insight
derived from the matter in hand itself — that prompted the method
of discussion, which consisted chiefly of stating what could be
stated together.[9] In the spirit of mutual trust, you can engage in a
dialog without either party being essentially and personally involved. There is, of course, much that can be said among separated
brethren and by separate theological traditions. Yet even the most
sincere endeavor of people to do such things together still does
not give them the courage to engage in a real dialog to the extent
of making a doctrinal statement. Such talk is, at best, the forerunner of a genuine dialog.

Ecumenical dialog at the deepest level, therefore, aims at the
reconciliation of the separated churches and the traditions which
they teach. There are many ways of taking the initiative in trying
to reach this goal. The most concrete phenomenon in this respect
is the attempt to reunite separate churches. It is normally preceded
by a long process of preparatory talks, clearing the ground. This,
in itself, involves considerable study of the theological funda-
mentals, which must then lead to final documents of reconciliation
as well as their expression in terms of worship. For fellowship in
the Eucharist should provide the framework of all theological study.
Although here and there in present day Christendom, sign posts are
erected on the road towards reconciliation, courage fails when it
comes to taking the further step towards a commitment to vital
dialog. Yet these signs are a call to the completion of visible church
unity.[10] Meanwhile, one of the ways to bring this about can still
be found in brotherly dialog, without worrying too much what
role this dialog is to play. Once the ecclesiological meaning of

dialog has been fully grasped, it can serve either as a continuing conversation without any precise definition of aim, or as an act of reconciliation, which by no means rules out the possibility of continued dialog. In each case, however, "dialog" will be interpreted differently. A dialog aimed at reconciliation cannot remain credible for long without the fellowship of the Eucharist. For the community of reconciled believers, genuine dialog not only prepares the way, but also acts as a constant companion along that way.

Theology in Dialog

This ecumenical situation has compelled theology to promote dialog between the different traditions. The various schools of thought have had to vindicate themselves in this confrontation with each other. It is no longer possible to identify truth with the tenets of one particular school of thought, or with the unbroken transmission of classical traditions. The simple confrontation with the existing differences have forced the parties concerned to take seriously the problem of unity and its correlative, the problem of binding truth. It stands to reason that these problems can be solved only by means of dialog.

Gospel and World. The question arises whether theology has derived any real help in its vital task from the dialog between previously established traditions. When consulting the sources of Christian revelation, we are confronted with the urgency of the problem of interpretation. The hermeneutic principles contained prior conclusions, which were by no means exclusively prompted by theological considerations. That is to say, theology in dialog proved of necessity to be interwoven with nontheological factors in exactly the same way as the problem of unity had done previously. This is not only due to method, but also due to material reasons. For although the specific questions which theology asks are concerned with salvation, surely they are first and foremost addressed to man and his world and beyond that, to the history of this world. Yet man, his world, and his history are not only objects of theological concern, but of scientific concern in general. In the course of its history, theology has enjoyed the strong links which have existed between it and the other sciences, although, in modern times, this relationship has had to find completely new forms of expression. For not only the scientific system, but also the (extratheological) insights into the world, man, and history throw up questions which have a bearing on theology.

These factors, very briefly outlined here, show up the ecumenically founded dialog of theology in the light of a wider context than it has been credited with in the past. A church-centered *oikoumene* endangers the recognition of truth by the church itself because, in too introverted a manner, it is concerned with a "world" which in reality does not even exist. It must be replaced by an *oikoumene* in which the church recognizes the world as the place and the goal of the gospel.[11] That being so, it follows that theology will have to be involved in the rediscovery of the necessary dialog with the world, and that the world will have to be drawn into the ecumenical discussion as an essential partner. Theological dialog therefore extends beyond the theological and ecclesiastical traditions to the "world," namely, to the pluralistic attitudes of mankind, and these must be acknowledged as partners in the dialog. The reason for this is not that the barriers between world and church have been eliminated. That would mean that the difference between message and receiver had been eliminated. Yet it is this differentiation which can no longer be made in the same way as it used to be made by traditional church teaching. The church itself must be seen as part of the world, and therefore must be drawn into the ambiguity of all that is worldly or secular. That dialog in which she thinks she is engaged within her own ranks, i.e., the dialog between the different Christian denominations, will necessarily and in fact turn out to be a dialog with the world. For her problems, especially those of unity and reconciliation, which are central to the whole of the ecumenical movement, are by no means isolated "ecclesiological" problems; they are directly related to the world; they are "secular" problems. Therefore, if you want to deal with them theologically, they must be related to the world in dialog.

The very demand for a theology of dialog is therefore motivated by theology itself. "The preacher must not merely address his fellow man with a general concern for the world around him; he must, in a true sense, catch up with him, he must include the alien, unaltered viewpoint in the event of the proclamation of the faith." [12] Only the question is what reason he gives for this "catching up"! We shall have to come back to this later on. Here, it must suffice to point to the necessity of maintaining the "otherness" of the world in theological dialog. The world must remain the world, even when it becomes a subject of theology. A "Christianized world" would no longer be in perspective, even if by that we mean no more than an offer to the world. To presuppose an "anonymous Christianity" as a basis for dialog would mean no more than a "churchification" of the world in modern disguise. Secularization has rightly arisen as a protest against this, and the new emphasis on the theology of creation has been a liberating influence in this respect.[13]

Theology in dialog must acknowledge the "otherness" of being and thinking, not only in the Christian, but especially in dialog with the world. It must allow its own insights to prove themselves in their encounter with this different way of thinking about the world, about man and about history. This does not imply that, from now on, "the world" will be the yardstick of theology, but that the message is addressed to the receiver as one who is living in this very world. For if the message, which is the subject of theology itself, already contains the receiver, man in this world,[14] he must be not merely a postulated, potential human being — or even one that has been thought up by the theologians, but real, historical man, as he has been known and described by the secular sciences. The situation in which he finds himself must be included in the scope of theological study.

Theology and Teamwork. A theology of dialog is thus faced with a gigantic task, which presumably cannot be tackled with the methods of traditional theological practice. You need only think of the tasks of exegesis, church history, doctrine, and ethics summarily in order to know immediately that those who do research in these disciplines can do so only to a very limited degree. If, to this, we add the increasing dependence of specialist theology on linguistics, philosophy, sociology, psychology, and history, the undertaking becomes even more complicated. This increasing challenge has lately been met within the sciences, including theology, by collaboration on innumerable collective projects. This tendency has made it necessary for the individual scholar to specialize. But here and there, an attempt is made to relate these individual fields of knowledge to one another. Therefore, it would surely be the most urgent task of dialog in theology, to foster this living relationship and thus to create a new vision of a wider *oikumene*. If it is true that, today, we are witnessing the evolution of a new dimension of thinking for the whole of mankind, then surely theology could make a considerable contribution to it. All the experiments which, in these days, are carried out by way of "team work" in the ecumenical movement, in theology in general and in the other sciences, would be greatly helped by being subjected to reflection at a deeper level. But that is precisely what can be done only by means of dialog. For if dialog essentially means relatedness, interdependence, and fellowship, then theology has a vital contribution to make.

Yet, strangely enough, the basis for theological team work has not even been taken up in ecumenical studies. It seems as though, in this respect, the only motivating factor has been the practical necessity of confronting the different traditions with one another. But how much this method could contribute to the knowledge of truth, and what exactly should be done to develop it methodically — these are questions which hardly anybody seems to have considered. This only underlines the urgency of the call for a theology of dialog.

In this context, we must further pose the question, whether a theology of dialog should presume to bring about a synthesis in which truth would be thought of as balanced and systematic. On the one hand, this question touches on the possible problem of a pluralism within theology itself. On the other hand, it could throw into critical relief another presumption which, in the course of history, has often been voiced, namely, the presumptuous claim of theology that it should have the final word of truth about man, about the world and about history. In a certain sense, these two problems are related to each other. Theology works in various fields. Its division into several disciplines could be seen simply as a practical issue. On the other hand, it could bring about a dialog within theology itself, provided that the specialization, which is often thought of wrongly as regrettable, is seen as a stimulus for embracing truth in all its different facets and as contributing to a common insight based on dialog. If that could be achieved, the insights of the different disciplines might not immediately demonstrate their unity, but their oneness might be shown up by merely being put in relationship with one another.

The repercussions of the different aspects pertaining to this insight could not fail to have an effect on theology. It is only in their isolation that one could perceive of them as disturbing. A variety of views within theology is not, in itself, a thing to be regretted. As long as, by means of dialog, it is possible to hold together a variety of tendencies and insights on the grounds of one and the same reality, the aim is not in danger of being satisfied with the lowest common denominator.[15]

If this is achieved, the relationship of theology with the other sciences hardly differs from the kind of variety we have been talking about. Truths about the history of our redemption would enjoy validity side by side with historic truths in general, in the same way as the truths of biblical and scientific anthropology. Theology does not put in the highest bid for insights of truth which have been gained outside its own sphere of study. On the contrary, the different departments (disciplines) of science make quite sure that every discipline studies reality with its own peculiar means and is not tempted to make pronouncements on matters which lie beyond its own capabilities. Dialog can, therefore, be considered as a precondition for the preservation of a genuine variety in theology and the sciences, without running the danger of paving the way for a "pluralistic" truth. The point of it is, rather, a variety of aspects, held together by the common bond of dialog. In this context, it must be mentioned that dialog is not a logical attempt to hold everything together dialectically in one and the same system: in dialog, a logical synthesis of the disparity caused by the differences is not even attempted.[16] After all, if we want to talk theology by means of dialog, we must first of all be willing to find the truth together in a fellowship which is mutual. "Dialectic" theology might be able to assert itself as the "system" of an individual theologian or even as a "school of theology." As distinct from this, a theology of dialog is, on principle, open-ended towards the other. You could even say that it calls for the complement of the other person's contribution. But, without exception, this is possible only where separate and yet basically inter-dependent people come together. We now want to examine what contribution such a theology can make in the search for truth.

THE DISCOVERY OF TRUTH IN THEOLOGICAL DIALOG

Is the discovery of truth through dialog at all possible? Could this not be a case of fundamental skepticism such as does, in fact, today rear its head in many different ways in the guise of "dialog"? Furthermore, if this is tolerated in recognition of the possibilities this offers for the discovery of truth, what kind of truth is this, especially when seen in relation to that which is gained through methods other than dialog? These are questions which we must seriously consider, especially since the problem of truth is of fundamental importance for theology.

The Reality of God and Our Statements of Truth

Reality confronts us as a mystery. As such, it is a challenge to any human endeavour of discovery. Yet, being a mystery, it is not simply the unknown, but the unknown in the known, namely, in all that presents itself to human endeavor as reality. In this way, every discovery becomes transcendent and is never able to stand still because, in probing into reality, it will always encounter the unfathomable and the incomprehensible. Once man begins to see the significance of the fact that no discovery can go beyond the limitations of the mind, and therefore begins to probe into the realm of existence — the understanding of being — he can do one of two things: either he identifies reality as God's reality or he does the opposite, he turns his discovery into an absolute. If he does the latter, he will end up by idolizing that reality which can be discovered and thus is accessible to man.[17] Yet even a mystery which cannot be identified holds within it God's presence (the presence of "the unknown God"), just as the arrogant claim of human reason to discern reality is bound to stand in awe and wonder when confronted with the "rustling leaf" (Luther).

The reality of God keeps the mystery. The Creator, though

"visible" in his works, remains the hidden and incomprehensible God. Man either worships him or batters himself to pieces on the rock of this mystery. Therefore there can be no theology which treats him as *deus nudus,* but theology must adhere to the manifest works of God, i.e., creation in the concrete sense of the word.

The reality of God as we see it in the incarnate Son, Jesus Christ, is no exception to this mystical nature of God. Even the claim that in this Jesus of Nazareth the promises of God have been fulfilled and that, in him, the New Covenant of the elect people of God has begun, remains a mystery. In rational terms, the fulfillment achieved by his suffering, death, and resurrection still contains within it the paradox of the "hidden" element within the revelation, and thus remains foolishness. God speaks to mankind, but the Logos, who is the instrument of his word, is a person, a destiny, an act of God. All that the spoken word can do is to interpret it, but notwithstanding the word of revelation, it remains a divine mystery. The reality of God is therefore a presence of the living God and not primarily the object of human talk. The one who proclaims, however, is the incarnate one who, through the preaching of his word, brings God's works to bear on man in the form of a promise.

This promise appeals not only to man's reason but to his faith, which alone is correlative to the divine initiative. The reality of God cannot be captured by the method of scientific evidence. Faith must affirm the reality of God before it is possible to know the mysteries of God. A fellowship of life and love must be born before knowledge can develop.[18] Otherwise, reason goes wrong and changes God's offer of grace into a destructive law which breaks man's back. For it is only by faith that man can perceive the reality of God as it is rather than as it appears to man.

Any knowledge of the reality of God, therefore, remains a waiting for enlightenment by God, who in his Son, through the Holy Spirit, leads us into all knowledge. Humans who listen to the revelation of God's word are addressed by God in human words. God's language is none other than the common language of human beings. In Holy Scripture, this language is spelled out for us in black and white. It is the means by which the Holy Spirit can use words and letters to give knowledge of the truth. Also, the prophetic and apostolic message uses human language in bearing witness to God and his works. The Old Testament is full of anthropomorphic statements about God, and similarly, in the New Testament, the sayings of Jesus about the kingdom of God take the literary form of the parable, the prophetic speech or the word of wisdom. These words of Jesus are accompanied by the works of his human existence, which "signify" all that the accompanying word wants to say. But the relation of the one to the other can only be disclosed by faith and trust in God. Yet neither the words nor the works of God are mere analogies of the "true" reality of God. For the mystery of God lies in the very fact that he is bringing his history, together with mankind, to completion in the human conditions of his incarnation. Long before the incarnation of Jesus Christ, God spoke to mankind in human conditions: his word reached men in the form of prophetic interpretation (rather than "from heaven") and demanded faith.

Theology is founded on revelation. Therefore it will be able to continue its work only as long as it respects the reality of God as a "hidden" mystery. It will not be able to presume the right to pronounce in direct speech on a mystery, when God's word itself does so in the "hiddenness" of human speech. Our dogmatic ideas can never be more than an "intention" of the truth, and therefore they can only try to describe the truth from ever new angles.[19] For this reason, a distinction has often been made between the intention of theological statements and their outward appearance. But in so doing, one runs the danger of devaluing the statement itself, as though it were irrelevant. In fact, the intention of every theological statement is the reality of God. But this reality reaches mankind by way of the word of revelation in history so that, although the theological statement and this reality are not identical, the latter cannot do without the word of revelation as interpreted by theology. As far as the possession of truth is concerned, theological insight can therefore only point to God's deeds, which are beyond the reach of man and thus remain a mystery. Any attempt at having the last and final word in doctrinal matters is bound to founder on the limitation of human insight.

We have seen that, between the reality of God and the correlative word of God on the one hand, and theological pronouncements of truth on the other, there is, of necessity, an area of latitude. It is within this area that theology must have the courage to work. Of course it can never disregard the fact that sin has corrupted reason. The multiplicity of expression must again and again be checked by the catharsis of God's word. At the same time, it need not cease to proclaim that aspect of truth which it has always so clearly promulgated, as long as it does not claim to have possession of the absolute truth.

Theological dialog will be able to spread in exactly this area of free play, which offers such a variety of possibilities, maintaining the element of mystery while daring to speak through theological insight and holding on to the faith in reality.

The Discovery of Truth by Means of Dialog

The theological witness to the truth of the gospel is in need of dialog. It is as we encounter reality in history, the world, and mankind that we grow in knowledge. We become consciously aware that this reality is of God only as we engage in dialog. Being led into the truth involves us in three visible respects: The way in which God acts and speaks to us points to dialog; as this dialog develops, truth unfolds itself by means of the historical process; and finally, what happens when we recognize that truth is spiritual.

God in Dialog with the World. The God of the Christian revelation is a God of relationships; and he can be known only because he established a relationship with the world. He has made himself known as the Creator and Redeemer of the world. That means that *any* knowledge is no less than a response to being known.[20] This essential relationship with God has been revealed to us as his love. Knowledge of God, therefore, is the loving relationship which God maintains in his dealings with the world, or if you like, in which he gives himself as love to the world. Christian theology is completely contrary to any kind of imaginary God who has set the world on its course and now watches its progress from the splendid isolation of his divine distance as a disinterested world judge. If that were so, any intellectual understanding of God's relationship in dialog would be impossible. For being known by God does not primarily consist of a table of contents, which has been transmitted to the world, to be pondered by mankind; it is a continuous act of God in his personal relatedness to the world, which took shape in the person of Jesus Christ. But at the same time, it is given "expression" in creation and in history by means of action in the world as well as through words. At the historical center of the world, God's action in the world takes concrete shape in the person of Jesus Christ, to whom everything in history has been pointing. In him, God received the name which had been kept secret from man. In him was made manifest God's glory which man had not been allowed to behold.

This action of God through history, with its focus in Jesus Christ, has the fundamental structure of dialog, in that it is intentionally aimed at man's knowledge. Witnessing to the work of God is our response to that action which is aimed at us. This knowledge is virtually a profession of him who reveals himself in his works and who has dealings with man long before he is professed by man. This witness is to be found in the Holy Scriptures of the Old and New Testaments: in the narrations of the historical and prophetic books, the action of history, open to all the world, is identified as God's history by the witness of faith. The national community, by virtue of its faithful witness, has a part in the creation of the narratives describing God's march through history as his dealings with mankind for the purpose of its preservation and redemption.[21] The history of the world calls for a fitting response. It is a challenge which man cannot ignore in the same way in which he might withdraw from the effects of an action aimed at him, into a realm where its impact cannot reach him and where he need not act in response to it. The fact that we are human means that we live on the level of a reality which is in dialog with us, whether we like it or not. Our life is a continuous acceptance of life, which comes to us as a gift.

Dialog, therefore, characterizes God's relationship with the world, not only by drawing man into the creative activity of God, but also by delivering God into the hands of man. Consequently, no man is without knowledge of God, even though that knowledge can be perverted. God, in his dialog with the world, remains the God of love who has manifested himself in the cross of Christ.

We are here touching on an important ingredient in the knowledge of God through dialog. This is the characteristic of communication which is inherent in knowledge, and which logically leads to dialog. Even in the old covenant, God used third parties, "mediators," who were his messengers in his dealings with men. He never met man "face to face," but chose to be "represented" by messengers in human form, or by his word in the guise of a human voice. He, himself, was present in this communication. He gave himself to man in the form of fellow men, or of their message. But then again, right at the center of history, God made his appearance among men in the form of the man, Jesus of Nazareth. In so doing, he placed himself into the hands of men, and they did not recognize him, precisely because they did not expect anything good to come "from Nazareth." Through this "mediator between God and man," however, truth was to be made known. It was possible to look at him as an ordinary rabbi because he spoke as a man. But in him, God kept hidden, and yet made possible, his existential dialog with man. Incarnation of God, therefore, means dealing with God through man, to talk to God by talking to a fellow man, to recognize God by being recognized by another human being. Our knowledge of God, thus, is given us by others, and is not the product of man-by-himself, who in any case is an illusion. I can be human only by what I have received from others, in whom my Creator and my life take effect.

The incarnate God sends his messengers into the world. They are his presence by passing on his word. The little ones are his presence, as in them, we respond to his call. Thus God is speaking to me when another person speaks to me; God deals with me in another person's dealings with me. His word comes to me not "from heaven" but from the world of men, and if I want to serve him I cannot by-pass my neighbor, but must serve God through him. God is in dialog with us through the world of human beings. Through it, he gives (or retains) his gifts to us, and through our attitude to the world, we accept (or despise) them. This relationship to God is concrete human reality. The way we treat that reality is the way we treat God.

Man, by receiving God's gifts, becomes himself a "mediator" of the Presence of God in the world. Not only does God's word and favor come to me through the other person, but through me, God himself goes out into the world, in word and in deed. Man proclaims the kingdom of God as one who has himself first received. The word of God comes to me through the testimony of the witnesses to the faith, both past and present. It cannot be absolved from this incarnation. The word, which is passed on by the one who proclaims it, was itself handed down as a "tradition" and therefore presupposes dialog between the various links in a chain of "tradition." It is not as though one individual link could possess knowledge of the gospel, but only in common with the others. The proclaimed word, stemming from the living dialog with the Fathers, now enters present-day history and challenges man to respond. Who, in this event, is the giver and who the receiver cannot be determined by rank or office. God is the one who proclaims, wherever men, engaged in dialog, share the word with one another.

The preacher in the world is himself a listener, or even a fellow-listener with the others, and therefore receives the word himself while passing it on. For he, himself, cannot be lonesome. He has been put among men in the world, and from the world he receives his daily livelihood by being creative. The word which proceeds from his lips is a word which has taken shape in a concrete, secular environment. For the "eternal" and "unchanging" word of God does not consist in the constant and unalterable nature of words, but in his faithful engagement in the concrete affairs of the world. It penetrates these affairs, illuminates them, and reveals them as God's history; the story of God's dealings with us, as a dialog of the existence of man, taking place on the initiative of God.

By allowing his word, proclaimed in this way, to be involved in each historical situation, God makes it the "unchanging" word: a word which bears witness to God's loving and faithful self-giving to mankind, the word of a God who visits the world as and where it is, at the right point in history. That is what is meant by God's dialog with the world. It is a dialog because God leaves the world to be itself, to have its own history, and directs his word right into it by depriving himself in the incarnation. This dialog of God with the world wants to find expression in the worship of the local Church.

Growth Towards Perfect Truth in Dialog. What God has done in Jesus Christ constitutes the revelation of the truth about man and the world. He is the truth and calls man to respond to him by means of a testimony, which gives verbal expression to his discovery of the truth. The Christian community worships a God who has engaged in dialog with the world. The confession of faith in a doxology is, therefore, the basic form of the theological discovery of the truth.[22] In the awe and wonder of believing, it expresses the fact that the church recognizes God as the Lord who is active within it. Wherever this doxology of the Church is heard, God's works have arrived at their goal, because they have been accepted. The doxology does not probe the mystery of God, but rather protects it. The Christian community does not understand the works of God any more than the rest of mankind. But by its worship, it gives God the praise, acknowledges him to be the One who acts, and thus bears witness to him in the world. The world is taught by this profession of the faith. Therefore it is of fundamental importance for theology to maintain the inseparable unity between the doxology and doctrine (in the liturgy as well as in *diakonia*) as the intellectual expression of the knowledge of God. For the doxology is an expression of faith and cannot be governed by the evidence of reason, although the intellect of man is certainly not excluded from worship. Only the relationship of the doxology to theological knowledge is a reflection of the vital difference between reality itself and our testimony of reality.

In Christ, there is the fullness of truth. He is God's perfect testimony of himself to the world. Whenever this truth is intellectualized, wherever it is separated from the doxology which professes this fullness, there you have a falsification of doctrine: the reality of God is reduced to the categories and limitations of human understanding and, although it transcends our understanding, is denied by it.[23] That, then, leads to man's claim to embrace in his teaching God's truth in its fullness. Knowledge of the truth, in such a case, is no longer determined by the fullness of Christ, but by the fullness of words with which the testimony is made. As though God in Christ had surrendered to our reason! Rather, the creative tension between the fullness of Christ and our knowledge of the truth must be maintained.

We should, of course, see Christ as the fullness of truth in the context of God's work in human history. For then, the fullness would not lie in the being centered on itself, but in the fullness of the presence of God — a presence that finds fulfillment in the process of history. The fullness of time, in which the revelation of Jesus Christ happened, is not timeless immutability but the physical entry of God into the world of time and space. That does not deny the progressive work of God in time; on the contrary, it gives it its full central meaning. Christ, as the personified fullness of God in this world, enters into the existence of this world. At the same time, he fulfills human existence and, with it, any human knowledge of the truth. *He* is the fullness, not the testimony *to* that fullness. In the process of history, the latter is subject to continual change as it arises from circumstance.

The fullness of truth, then, must always be seen in the whole context of the historical process of truth itself.[24] The doxology is the appeal of this fullness to the world. Theology, however, is the historical reflection of this fullness in man's understanding. Although, therefore, concrete theological testimony can lay claim to this fullness of Christ, it is nonetheless in varying degrees subject to the historical growth of knowledge. In every historical situation, this fullness of truth manifests itself and formulates the gospel in its encounter with Jews, Greeks, and pagans in different forms of expression, each of them related to the one and only fullness in Jesus Christ, and yet overlapping with one another. It is in this fullness that they are one, not in the form of their testimony. It follows that increase in knowledge does not mean a dissection of the fullness of Christ into separate little portions for human consumption. Surely, at any point in time, in a greater or smaller measure of knowledge, there is always one and the same fullness, and this — the perfect and complete presence of Christ — is both the driving force and the authority behind the testimony. Whether, therefore, it is "milk" or "solid food" that is being offered, the fullness of the testimony depends on its relation to Christ. The different forms do not fall apart on account of their different positions in some scale of values, but they derive their particular value from the fullness of Christ.[25] Consequently, growth in Christian knowledge is fed by faith in the mystery of this fullness in the field of historic reality.

The foregoing does, in fact, describe the nature of dialog in its relation to theological knowledge and discovery. For, invariably, dialog depends for its life on a common affirmation which, in the case of theology, can only be the fullness of Christ. On the ground of this affirmation, expressing as it does certainty of faith in belonging to truth itself, there grows brotherly exchange according to the respective measure of insight. The primitive Christian liturgy was the event at which the different members of the church shared with one another whatever measure of knowledge they had received. Thus, the foundation of dialog is the fellowship of the ecclesia. The ontological fact of being "incorporate" in the body, together with the experience of sharing with one another, enables us to grow in knowledge. This growth consists, not only in a straightforward germination of truth from a common seed, but also in whatever correction each may receive from the other to offset the danger of falling away from the fullness of truth. But here it must be noted that dialog derives from fellowship with others through the fullness of Christ and *not* from a greater or lesser measure of knowledge. Because the fellowship exists in the *pleroma*, dialog induces growth "to the measure of the stature of the fullness of Christ," to mature manhood (Eph. 4:13-16). Within the body, the differences are given according to the measure of knowledge and are used in the exchange of dialog for upbuilding itself in love. That is why the fullness of Christ can never be "institutionalized": it is concurrent with growth, and not identical with a deposit of faith, from which "new things and old" can be extracted according to requirement. Rather, all knowledge is an event of communication, founded on the fullness of Christ.

Truth as a Pneumatic Event in Dialog. Truth is an event, which in dialog expresses itself by means of the spoken word. It is given as the fullness of Christ, but it enters concrete human existence, in that it happens between human beings in the form of dialog. For this reason, truth, as it is recognized in dialog, is something ever new, surprising, unexpected. This is because it is not our doing: it is given.

Dialog would be quite futile if truth were, from the start, in the possession of this or that partner. If that were so, it would merely have to be passed on from the one to the other. Or you might imagine that the partners in dialog agree, in each case, to exchange their own measure of truth (or appropriate aspect of it) among each other. But this would be no more than the technical procedure of registering what had already been there in the first place, and the so-called "dialog" would then mean precisely nothing in terms of discovering the truth. This would obviate the necessity for a technical dialog in the sense of a conversation with different partners: the respective information could be incorporated in my self-made treasury of truth by means of mechanical transmission (in writing or through a would-be messenger).

Real dialog, however, starts from the premise that something vital happens between the partners in the dialog concerning their knowledge of the truth itself. The whole point of it is to expect from the dialog the epiphany of truth itself. There is no question here of attempting a synthesis, producing out of two preexisting experiences of truth yet another, a third one. That would still be no more than a feat of rational aptitude. The dissolution of a dialectic formula by means of a synthesis is not a dialog but a process of logic. Dialog is a spiritual event, in which profound encounter leads man to perceive reality as truth itself, rewarding his expectation by letting something happen *between* him and his partner. No room here for the self-sufficient observation that "my" truth is vindicated or is instrumental in moulding a new discovery of truth! All we can observe here is that what has happened between the partners in dialog is truth itself.

This unpredictable "between" in dialog is the moment of the Spirit, is his opportunity to create something new and to lead us to a knowledge of the truth by our being known of the Spirit himself.[26] Thus you are brought to the perception of a third person's presence in the dialog. This presence is the fulfillment of the promise for two or three who are gathered together in the name of Jesus. But it is precisely through the presence of Jesus that it becomes a pneumatic event, the fulfillment of the promise that God would send the Holy Spirit. This happens in the dialog between those who wait for him as the Spirit of truth, who will lead them to the knowledge of the truth.[27] In the dialog before the face of

God the miracle happens: that which could never have happened to man in his self-sufficiency and in his isolation with "his" truth, now happens in his dialog with his partner, while together they live from the presence of the third person and listen to him. Through the *Pneuma Christi* they partake of reality.

Now, this can give rise to the fear that dialog might result in the loss of one's own personality. After all, in a synthesis you can still somehow rediscover and uphold your own jealously guarded component of knowledge; but if the new element which comes to those engaged in dialog is identified as the presence of Christ's Spirit, then your self clearly seems to be eliminated.[28] Such an argument can only be countered by questioning the anthropological premise on which it is based; that of the individual self in isolation. That is to say, the human being as a person does not exist other than in relationship with other human beings. Only in his encounter with his fellow humans does he become himself. What matters here is not primarily the social nature of man but the nature of genuine humanity; and it is this humanity which enables me to recognize my own personal being in relation with the others. What I am can only be understood from the standpoint of the other person. It follows that my personal being becomes an entity only when I stand face to face with God, which does not exclude, but include, my standing face to face with other people. "Man becomes an 'I' through the 'Thou'" (M. Buber).[29] He destroys himself by denying this relationship. A self which cannot be opened up by another, i.e., a self that does not admit of a "between" of human existence in dialog, can only perish in its fanatical delusion.[30] Genuine self-realization happens when man is open towards the reality of the universe and prepared to receive himself, i.e., the truth about himself, as a present, by partaking of reality in the pneumatic event. Dialog is nothing but the method, or the self-evident way of leading man to the knowledge of the truth through the pneumatic presence of Christ.

Dialog offers a third choice over and above individualism and collectivism. It is creative. Individualism is not absorbed into an amorphous collective something, but neither is it thrown back on itself: it is carried by a body, in which the members, endowed with the gift allotted to them by the Spirit, and belonging to each other, play their part "for the common good." Knowing the truth is, therefore, not the privilege of a solitary individual sitting in the midst of the congregation, endowed with a charisma. Rather, the individual is incorporated in the community of that knowledge, which the different members impart to one another. It is in the dialog of the different charismata, in the give-and-take, in the doxology of hymns, of exhortation, of witness, of prophecy, that the knowledge of truth is given. By directing love towards the edifying of the body, the one spirit holds everything together and gives life in the truth.

Knowledge of the truth within the community of Jesus Christ is dependent upon this vital dialog of the members one with another. The ecclesia recognizes the Lord, professes him, and proclaims him to the world. Theology cannot absolve itself from this condition for the Christian's knowledge of the truth. Its own life depends on this knowledge through dialog, and it can therefore only conceive its task as that of a *koinonia* of truth.[31] That is what gives the theologians' cooperative work a deeper significance than an occasional technical "teaming up" for group work. For if the knowledge of truth is a pneumatic event in dialog, this indicates that theology does not live from isolated feats on the part of individuals, but has its proper place in the dialog of the ecclesia. This, in turn, would deepen the scientific evidence for the fact that each individual result in theology is intertwined with the work of innumerable fellow-workers in the big theological enterprise. The historian may trace the genesis of each theological insight; he may indicate cause and effect in the relationship between teacher and disciple; he may point out schools of thought and theological tendencies; yet the miracle of genuine dialog can only be perceived in the pneumatic presence. The new element in a person's insight into truth, likely to become evident at any moment, cannot be identifiable with the evidence of reason — in fact, for the purposes of such an analysis, there is hardly anything entirely new in it. It is like a present, accessible to the recipient only — but to him, it is given quite suddenly as the new entity, in which he may take part.

The question confronting all who are engaged in theological work in our generation is this: are we not called once again to take this factor of truth in dialog into account and to put more faith into it rather than in the possibility of balancing off the different schools of thought with one another by means of logic? For truth recognized in dialog makes for fellowship. It can stand its own intrinsic tensions, because it derives its life from the fact of "being together." Dialog* transcends the boundaries of logic — it becomes the ground of existence for a thinking community.[32] The ecumenical dimension of thinking is the truth which confronts us. It is only through the fellowship of thought that the theological thinker becomes aware of his own innermost thoughts. The method of dialog evokes insights, such as can only be brought to light in their whole import, in their consequences and in their hidden potential, by these means. The way the insights of the individual are thus illuminated is a certain proof of the fact that truth is not at the disposal of the individual, but is given through dialog.

A theologian who bases his work on the doxology will, in the midst of his endeavor to find out the truth, call on the Holy Spirit to intervene on his behalf. His call for the Holy Spirit is, rightly, the call for a partner in dialog, for the fellow-being and the fellow-thinker in the realm of truth. He is called into the fellowship of truth by the fathers and brothers of the past and the present, by putting himself into this fellowship and by calling, in his turn, the others. Thus dialog becomes the mutual communication of truth, as the Holy Spirit takes hold of man by means of his truth and as he makes that man the mouthpiece of that truth. The call for truth is basically linked with the means of grace, the charismatic gifts. The truth is not an abstract word of God, but a living word professed with human lips. In dialog, man is calling for this instrument of the Holy Spirit and is unconsciously offering himself as the instrument of his own insight. The result is a communication of truth through the variety of insights, and in an hour of grace the word of life is given, without anybody's being able to tell from where it comes and where it will go. As a pneumatic event, truth, in the Christian's insight, is under the merciful hand of God. Partners in dialog intercede for one another, that the truth may happen in their midst.

Dialog as a Refining Influence in the Discovery of Truth. Truth

---

* Germ. "Dialogik" meant here as a pun: "dia-logik" transcends the boundaries of "Logik" (translator's note).

is the reality of God himself. It is accessible through God's work in the world both as a revealed and as a hidden reality. It is received, but at the same time it can be rejected. In the cross of Christ, this truth has been erected in the sight of the world. It puts mankind at the crossroads. All are under the domination of sin and of untruth; and all have been called by the gracious work of God to take part in the truth of the new aeon. All men have been given the promise that the Holy Spirit will lead them into all truth. But how is that going to happen?

Dialog as a Conflict Between Truth and Untruth. That God's truth appeared in the person of Jesus Christ is not entirely convincing for the world. For mankind, through its disobedience towards God, has fallen a victim to untruth. Jesus Christ, through his struggle against the forces of the enemy, is redeeming man from his fall to false images. He enters the palace of "the father of lies" and overcomes him from within. The victory is given, but only in the hiddenness of the cross. The resurrection reinstates life, and the truth of God, by the power of the Holy Spirit and by the authority of this victory, is historically intertwined with this. Truth and untruth are at war with one another, just like the spirit and the flesh. The victory gained by Christ does not mean that untruth is immediately eradicated from the world, but the two are to stand side by side towards the final eschatological conflict. The kingdom of God and the kingdom of Satan are in conflict with each other until the day of judgment, when the truth about the world will be revealed finally and irrevocably. Until then, the search for truth will continue to mean an on-going struggle against untruth. Therefore we must put all that we have just found out about the discovery of truth as a pneumatic event, into this context.

If the help of the Holy Spirit is promised for the discovery of the truth, then this help cannot be separated from the struggle for truth in this our age. In that case, dialog about the truth reveals itself as such a struggle, and its nature can be told from the existential situation of the simultaneousness of the two aeons.

That, in turn, means that the interwovenness of truth and untruth cannot be unravelled by a logical process of separation. The victory of truth does not exactly run like a straight line through the course of history. There is an indissoluble coexistence of truth and untruth.

But it is not a peaceful, it is a frightening kind of coexistence, forever overcoming itself and refining the insight into truth. The help of the Holy Spirit, furthermore, is not the promise of a logical knowledge of the truth in its pure form. It is the promise that in this struggle, the truth will never perish but will prove victorious against all appearances. The eschatological victory of truth is already present today as, in dialog, truth defeats untruth among those people who search for it.

Dialog, therefore, must not be thought of as some innocuous entity enabling truth to embark upon its march through history in a straight and uninterrupted line. Certainly, dialog is not a debate, a dispute, in which the arguments of one partner win over those of the other, or even force the other to his knees. In dialog, the word of truth is passed on from the one to the other by means of a secret runway. The success of truth does not consist in my uncovering the untruth of the other, but to bring to light those grains of untruth which are hidden within my knowledge. For the revelation of truth is not possible but through the revelation of my own untruth. Here, the partner in dialog is the tool, to raise my untruth to the level of consciousness and in that very way, to convince me of the truth. That is to say, the truth which attains validity in my own knowledge is in need of being purified through the process of dialog. After all, I do not possess the truth. Rather, it comes towards me, in a straight line, from the other person; and as I myself am still living in the flesh, the permeation of my existence by truth cannot come about before untruth in me has been overcome.

This is where the Holy Spirit comes to our aid, so that we do not perish in this struggle. But he does not promise a straightforward victory. The detours in the progress of our salvation also apply to our understanding of the truth.[33] The element of unity in one's understanding of the truth does not lie in its undisturbed, continuous development. The idea of a quiet undisturbed development of dogma goes right against the grain of our situation when viewed from the angle of the history of our salvation. A theology of dialog is capable of utilizing this insight for our understanding of the truth. It will have to see dialog as a clash between truth and untruth, and it will not be able to think of truth in down-to-earth doctrinal statements as independent from interference by untruth.[34] It will have to concede that untruth can even enter into our statements of truth. Truth cannot simply indicate the border-lines against untruth, but true understanding will always be partly conditioned by an aspect of untruth. Not even corrections of untruth are always free from the premises of the same, and can therefore maintain their content of truth only within the limitations of their own situation, i.e., only by means of dialog with untruth. If anybody tried to make them into a never-changing formula of truth, they would betray truth.

Understanding of the truth is by nature linked with dialog — something that progresses from the conflict of history, not something that is given in a cumulative development, forever completing and perfecting itself. Growth in understanding is not an understanding which grows quantitatively, but a continuous, historically conditioned confrontation, a conflict between reality and the understanding of man as conditioned by space and time. The help of the Holy Spirit is given in this conflict of understanding by enabling truth at all times to become articulate and, by a realization of faith, also to be perceived. It lies within its own natural propensity towards conflict that this understanding of truth is kept from institutionalizing the help of the Holy Spirit. Institutions are no protection against error. All who are called to search for truth are in danger of falling into error, and it is only the promise that truth will win which enables them to face that danger. We do not possess the truth; it possesses us. We are reminded of this by our fragmentary knowledge and our deceptive deviations, such as only dialog reveals them. That is why every insight into truth bears the mark of forgiveness and is received in the full trust that the march of truth towards victory will be completed.[35]

It follows that a theology of dialog must lead to a revision of the traditional criteria for what is or is not "heresy." Although the pronouncement of an anathema has hardly ever been directed against definite individuals or communities, excommunications did normally concern individual people. You might say that heresy trials were always concerned with the salvation of the heretic. Yet they were directed against individuals or groups of people whom they excluded from the fellowship of truth, unless, of course, those concerned had in advance pronounced their anathema against their excommunicators.[36] The struggles for truth among Christians have led to those divisions which, in the course of history, seem to have increased rather than decreased. If the brutality of that struggle has come to an end, then it is only because the other side lacks the means of destruction, or one's own side has grown a little more humane — and this has given rise to greater tolerance. But that does not mean that the problem of the traditional way of dealing with heresy has been overcome. That way is questioned radically only where you have a theology of dialog.

In assessing heresy, people have largely started with the premise that it can be identified as a straightforward untruthfulness, as a denial of the truth of Christ. Sentence was passed against it on the ground of a truth which was just as unambiguously conceived to the exclusion of the other side of the coin. It would be facile to try and solve this problem of the gulf between truth and nontruth by means of a theological pluralism, allowing different thought forms to contain a common measure of truth.[37] That this possibility exists is, today, a theological commonplace. It was, however, necessary for us to adduce the interwoven nature of truth and untruth, in order to clarify the problem of heresy from the very core of the discernment of truth.

We have described dialog as the struggle of truth against untruth, warning against the division of the opponents in such a way as to enable the one or the other to prove itself in its pure form by means of rational evidence. In dialog, truth stands in the no-man's-land between the conflicting partners, i.e., it is not to be found with the one or the other, but it happens — in concrete thought forms, of course — between the partners. The position regarding untruth is similar. That is why the "truth partner" cannot in safety possess his deposit of faith in the vessels of his intellect without being convicted even by the "untruth partner" of a disguised form of treason against truth. Yet even the challenge of the "untruth partner" contains within it an element of truth. The "truth partner" is called to grant him that truth. It lies, therefore, in the nature of this dialog to follow up each aspect of truth in the respective views (on both sides), to acknowledge it, and from there, to unfold that truth, which both of them hold in common. For it may be in the protest against "my" testimony to the truth that truth itself is active. Also, the enemy of my concept of the truth has the right to have truth granted to him. For although he may adhere only to one aspect, this may nonetheless be true in itself, when viewed from the wider testimony to the truth.[38] Dialog looks for this truth in the partner, be he ever so "mistaken," and in his affirmation of this knowledge, nobody, can claim the victory, but must cede it to the truth. Theology of dialog must, therefore, be possessed by the desire to convince the other partner, not of the untruth of his position, but of the truth of the position he himself is striving for. That is what establishes and maintains fellowship in the discovery of truth. Within such a working relationship, with each helping the other and both supporting one another in the discovery of truth, the common task will be to create the openness for the event of truth itself.

Once conflict in dialog is admitted to be part of its nature, it is virtually impossible to exclude from it the "enemy" of that truth which we ourselves have come to see. To put it less abstractly: a theology of dialog will feel compelled to pay attention also to those who do not want to live on the basis of truth as revealed in Jesus Christ as the reality of God, but who contradict it.[39] For according to the evidence of history, God's truth is not only proclaimed by the faithful, but also through his enemies. His people are called back to the truth by God through the criticism of such "outsiders." For that reason, theology cannot be content with a dialog within its own specialized circle, but must listen to the world — not only with regard to its history, but also to its interpretation by those who have been alienated from the Christian faith. It follows that the world is an essential partner of the theology of dialog.[40]

In the present age, we have become more and more theologically aware of the fact that the works of the world are the works of God, no matter whether they are done by a believer or by a non-believer. If evil works are allowed in history, we can recognize in them the wrath of God, who through the work of demons, calls men to repentance. We are, however, not yet used to hearing God speak to us through the voice of unbelief, although the early church fathers often affirmed this insight in a positive way. The dialog between believers and unbelievers, then, cannot be excluded from the dialog between God and his people about truth itself. We cannot here go into detail about the effect this will have on a truly ecumenical (= world-wide) theology.[41] But as far as our so-called ecumenical dialog is concerned, the immediate consequences of all this cannot be shelved. Let us touch on them at least in the form of a question: is not the reason for most of the divisions in the different Christian traditions that the insights of any given age (naturally?) cannot embrace all the vital aspects of reality? The correction arising from each given situation, which had within itself genuine statements of truth, might well have proved itself as a partner in dialog. But how is it that so many of these corrections have tried to assert themselves as independent entities? [42] Only because the other side rejected them, or because they themselves wanted to make absolute statements of truth, thus barring the way towards genuine dialog?

Today, we are on the threshold between two dimensions of thought: monolog and dialog. But does not that mean that we are also confronted by the necessity for resolving the tensions arising from Christian insights into truth by means of dialog within the same great community of thought, of facing up to the need to fight for the cause of truth, if need be, yet without necessarily identifying our own knowledge of truth with the boundaries of that great community of the like-minded? If that is so, then a theology of dialog could be a means of generating greater enthusiasm for an attitude which would not exclude insights into truth such as belong to the community, yet in dialog would not constitute a threat to truth. The inherent risk that truth itself would thus be exposed to the dangers of perversion must be accepted.

The Limitations of Dialog in the Field of Theology. In what has been said so far about the interwoven nature of truth and untruth, and in subscribing to the idea that truth proves its real quality in its struggle with untruth, we must not lose sight of the fact that there is a clear dividing line between truth and untruth. Yet in the field of a theology of dialog, this dividing line takes a course different from what we would normally expect. For one thing, it is much more clearly marked than it would be in monolog.

It is the hallmark of a theology of monolog to shield truth by subjecting it to strict isolation. Such a theology claims to have seen the truth — and from this stronghold position, it thinks it can repel the onslaught of untruth by all means. Thus dialog is made to feel its limitations by being rejected. It is thought to be in the interests of truth that dialog is banned. In its place, there are put the methods of monolog, namely, polemics and controversy with an opponent, who only exists according to the dictates of "my" understanding, but who may not speak in his own cause.

We do not want to belittle the intellectual integrity of the polemic or controversial theologian, nor his sincere endeavor to be fully informed of the other person's point of view. But he does not listen sincerely to the other person, because the latter appears to him as the enemy of truth, who must be contradicted. You must not expect to hear the word of truth from him; at best, you can grant him that, seen subjectively, he is honest.[43] But his word cannot get through to me, because the truth has been localized on my own side. It follows that monolog is intellectual fanaticism which, together with an ecclesiological attitude of mind, acts as a midwife to all anathemas. Wherever the dialog between different traditions cannot be sustained (even if it takes a very primitive, i.e., technically informative form), the in-breeding of a so-called truth sets in, leading to a perversion of the truth which, as we have seen, can only prove itself in dialog. Of course, we do not want to deny that also a theology based on monolog has achieved a good many things which still cannot be ignored today. But, amazingly, this theology becomes significant only to the degree in which it is subjected to dialog, that is, in which it is no longer accepted simply as an insight into truth based on monolog.

So it is that truth itself compels us never to interrupt the dialog. For wherever it is broken off, there is a treason against truth itself, which cannot live in isolation. It is a conversation with the world, even the world of untruth, and in each case, it derives its formula from this encounter in dialog. If you break off a dialog, you owe the other person, even if he is your opponent or enemy, the truth, and (what is perhaps even more amazing!) you owe yourself the truth, seeing that it can only come to you and reach your conscious thinking through the other person. You can, therefore, argue the case for dialog from the standpoint of catholicity.[44] However, the truth which is all-embracing (i.e., catholic) must not be looked upon as a given property or lead to a claim similar to that made by monolog.[45] Openness for dialog is the ingenuousness of faith. It contains the certainty that truth has its own resources and can assert itself.

It is only in dialog that the frontiers of truth can be clearly distinguished. All that happens in the dialectic method is that various lines of thought are commissioned to bring about the desired synthesis. In dialog, the different views have their own, indigenous commission. While in monolog, thoughts are suppressed or kept silent in favor of the dominant idea, and while in dialectics they are considered only lightly by the criterion of a future synthesis, dialog opens up the freedom of thought in the recognition of truth.[46] From the point of view of dialog, nothing is without interest, not even untruth. Yet one must not go so far in one's interpretation of the freedom of dialog as to think of truth itself as being pluralistic. The insights by which men come to express truth take many different forms. They differ from one another in their thought form, but also in their content, to such an extent that it seems almost futile to try and bring them into harmony with one another. Dialog is the attempt to sustain the varied nature of these insights side by side with each other. It is not resignation in the face of many possible truths as they will exist in a pluralistic society. It has its ontological foundation in reality, which is recognized in theology as God's reality, and therefore necessarily presents itself as a reality which cannot be contained by the insights of human reason.

Reality itself is that which has been given from the first: it is there even before dialog begins and insights can be formed. Although there is a variety of insights, they are all related to the one reality, in which they are united — perhaps even without having any concrete rational evidence. To presuppose this all-embracing unity is not synonymous with a relapse into monolog. You might even call it a necessity, if the insights are not to create multifarious chaos. The affinity of insights as demonstrated in dialog has its ontological ground in the unity which holds this reality together.

It is therefore not sufficient, in order to account for the success of human thinking, to state that each conscience is able to comprehend all the knowable. It must be admitted that all consciences, as a whole, are dominated, influenced, oriented by a kind of higher Conscience, who animates, controls, synthesizes the taking possession of the universe by each individual monad. Not only is each of us partly All, but all of us are taken and coalesced into a unifying togetherness. There is a Center of all centers, a Center without which the whole structure of thought would crumble away into dust.[47]

The Christian faith even dares identify this center of consciousness in the universe with the living God, without thereby inflicting a presupposition on the dialog. Also, where God is looked upon as the one who unifies all the humanly unsettled and immature views, dialog is fully subscribed to.

The God of dialog would thus be the God of the *coincidentia oppositorum* as well, whose transcendence contradicts the inherent limitation of human condition. Dialog allows either contrary to express itself, meaning that convergence if not coincidence must be realized on a higher level of intelligence. The unity of dialog rests in the community of common intention, in the common viewing of the point at the horizon where the parallels, which by their inner law are kept apart, at least meet ideally.[48]

Dialog is a relationship to a center in which those taking part are one — that ought to be the basic premise of every dialog. The theology of dialog cannot tear itself away from the revelation of God without ceasing to exist as *theo*logy. The theological motivation of dialog will always have its roots in this: that when human partners engage in dialog there is another One who is active, and he has promised his presence through his Holy Spirit. What happens between those engaged in dialog is, therefore, at the same time, something *extra nos,* to which dialog can contribute precision of definition: *sed non sine nos.* The Holy Spirit gives himself through his own means, which include human instruments, to make possible his work in our midst. If the theologian counts on this reality, he is placed altogether differently from the person who is bent on the method of rational evidence belonging to the mathematician's and physicist's concept of reality. The theology of dialog is *meta-*

physical in the sense that it does not deduce reality from the analysis of the world as accessible to reason, or identify it with the latter. Rather, it counts on creative influence in being at work in the world which, despite human cooperation, is indisposable — in fact, it even disposes of us. A theology of dialog which is content with embracing only that which is in existence, that which is evident in its multiplicity, would be basically materialistic, even if it exercised this method by means of the offered subject matter of theological insights.[49] The theology of dialog therefore draws a sharp distinguishing line between an intellectualization of dialog and an attitude that is basically existential and cannot be derived from its own resources, but holds to dialog as a transcendent reality.

Although it is true that the theology of dialog draws the lines of demarcation for insight very clearly, it is under no obligation to insist on the same conditions for its partner. In down-to-earth dialog, it will be seen whether any other conditions will be able to stand. On different planes,[50] only one basis for dialog must be found, which can serve as the premise for the development of dialog in each case.

It is in the nature of dialog that it should help theology keep its own identity, but that it admits to the freedom for other ways of gaining knowledge and insights. The present-day sympathy and understanding surrounding dialog gives theology the opportunity of fulfilling its mission in a wider field, and even to receive much more help towards the fulfillment of its mission than has been possible until now. The evolution of dialog in theology allows us a hopeful look towards the future in the ecumenical movement, which bursts the fetters of ecclesiastical and theological traditions and extends into the universe as a reality belonging to God.

Today, when there is such a call for dialog, the theology of dialog has a particular mission. It can attach a hope to the method of dialog, which represents its peculiar calling: to voice the presence of God in the dialog between the sciences and in all that happens between humans engaged in dialog.

> Let us say it freely: in the new world, faith proves to be less and less transferable as truth, according to all that traditionally can be considered as normal. More and more it is born as a result of an "encounter." As Jean-Claude Barreau has

pointed out in a beautiful testimony, it is Emmaus which has to be added to this investigation. Emmaus has become the central symbol for so many unbelievers today: the sudden appearance of the one whom they had thought to be dead. Perhaps we ought to follow on in this direction, if we want to leave this time of darkness in the history of faith. For the latter no longer seems to be the painful privilege of a handful of mystics, but is assuming a firm dimension: to bother less about adapting the message, about modernizing the institutions, about taking up the threads of history at the point at which the church failed — rather, to live as though we were hearing the word for the first time. . . .[51]

— Translated by W. B. Muller

NOTES

1. On the subject of "Dialog as Theological Method," cf. *Oecumenica* 1969, *An Annual Symposium of Ecumenical Research,* Minneapolis, Minn., 1969.
2. Cf. my contribution "Zur ekklesiologischen Bedeutung des Dialogs," *ibid.* p. 11-27.
3. In the following, we therefore make several statements in which we differentiate between truth itself and the discovery of truth. In this, we differ from H. L. Goldschmidt, *Dialogik, Philosophie auf dem Boden der Neuzeit,* Frankfurt, 1964, to whom we are greatly indebted in this study. Goldschmidt has turned the pluralistic concepts of truth into "different truths" and "controversial" philosophizing into an "unavoidable necessity, which extends as far as philosophy's own contradiction of religion" (p. 13). The one and only universe as it has been made known to us today, can only be expressed by means of "two concepts . . . , which are different truths, and yet true" (p. 11).
4. Teilhard de Chardin emphasized this very strongly. cf. e.g., his essay "L'atomisme de l'esprit," *Oeuvres,* vol. VII, Paris, 1963, pp. 43-45. "Henceforth, and more than ever, man will have to accept that he no longer thinks by himself. . . . That which thinks already, as well as that which works, through man and over beyond him is once again a Humanity."
5. Cf. Teilhard de Chardin's terms *"co-réflexion, hyper-réflexion, mega-synthèse,"* etc., which are always linked with terms of personalization (also hyper-personalization).
6. Such a "Personalism in Dialog" has been presented among contemporaries chiefly by the Jewish thinker M. Buber. See especially the two volumes: *Dialogisches Leben,* Zürich, 1947, and *Das dialogische Prinzip,* Heidelberg, 1965, in which his most important writings on the problem of dialog have been presented afresh.
7. At the Faith and Order Conference in Lund, 1952, this problem of the one-sided confessional method of obtaining information was explained by E. Schlink and O. Tomkins. See the official report: *The Third World Conference on Faith and Order,* London, 1953, pp. 150-173.

8. See, e.g., the report of Section I in *The First Assembly of the World Council of Churches*, ed. by W. A. Visser 't Hooft, London, 1949, p. 53 f.

9. The united theological studies, which began after the World Conference in Lund, concentrated on working out common ground on the basis of Scripture. What was more difficult, was to evaluate the actual conclusions drawn from the biblical evidence for the purposes of the practical ecumenical situation, in which the churches found themselves. Cf. Edmund Schlink, "Die Methode des dogmatischen ökumenischen Dialogs," in *Kerygma und Dogma*, 1966, pp. 205-211; and P. E. Persson, "Dialog als theologische Methode" in *Oecumenica* 1969, pp. 120-129.

10. J.-L. Leuba is right in saying that genuine ecumenical dialog can only take place "within the ecumenical sphere." Cf. *A la découverte de l'espace oecuménique*, Neuchâtel, 1967, p. 219.

11. The Lutheran-Roman Catholic dialog on "Gospel and Church" had to include this "third partner" — the world — in their deliberations with remarkable promptness. In so doing, it opened up the missionary dimension of dialog. In this connection, cf., the report of A. Hasler and H. Meyer in *Lutheran World* 1969, esp. p. 372 f.

12. H. U. von Balthasar, "Die Einheit der theologischen Wissenschaften," in *Hochland*, München, 1968, p. 700.

13. E. Schillbeeckx, "L'unique témoignage et le dialogue dans la rencontre avec le monde," in *Oecumenica* 1969, p. 173 f.

14. This was worked out as a basic theme in *Die Predigt*, München, 1959, by G. Wingren.

15. Cf. K. Rahner, "Pluralism in Theology and the Unity of the Church's Profession of Faith," in *Concilium*, vol. 6, No. 5, London, 1969, pp. 49-58.

16. H. L. Goldschmidt, "Dialektik oder Dialogik — eine notwendige geistige Entscheidung," in *Internationale Dialog Zeitschrift*, 1969, pp. 194-208 has rightly pointed this out.

17. A. E. Loen, in his excellent study on Secularization, rightly rejected as unscientific the emphasis on a concept of reality which exclusively uses the mathematical-physical method. (*Säkularisation. Von der wahren Voraussetzung und angeblichen Gottlosigkeit der Wissenschaft*, München, 1965).

18. Pascal pointed out in an impressive way that divine truths reach man's mind via his heart, and not vice versa. "The saints, on the contrary (viz., as distinct from rational pride), will say, when speaking of divine matters, that one must love these matters in order to know them, and one enters into truth only through charity..." ("De l'art de persuader," in *Oeuvres complètes*, Ed. du Seuil, Paris, 1963, p. 355).

19. P. Y. Congar is fond of pointing out a patristic saying quoted by Thomas ab Aquino, in which an article of faith is described as "perceptio veritatis tendens in ipsam," (S.Th. II-II, q 1 a 6 sed c).

20. Cf. J. Dupont, *Gnosis. La connaissance religieuse dans les épitres de Saint Paul*, Bruges-Paris, 1949.

21. On Old Testament historical writings as an expression of faith in God, cf. G. von Rad, *Old Testament Theology*, vol. I, pp. 154 ff., where this is emphasized for the profane, humane, and de-sacralized history.

22. Cf. F. Kattenbusch, *Die Entstehung einer christlichen Theologie,* New edition, Darmstadt, 1962; and E. Schlink, "The Structure of Dogmatic Statements as an Ecumenical Problem," in *The Coming Christ and the Coming Church,* Philadelphia, 1968.

23. E. Schlink has recently drawn attention to this structural change of Christian dogma in "The Unity and Diversity of the Church," in *What Unity Implies,* ed. R. Groscurth, Geneva, 1969, p. 33 f.

24. The connection between the term "fulfill" *(pleroun)* and "build up" *(oikodomein)* has been outlined by H. Ljungman, *Das Gesetz erfüllen,* Lund, 1954, e.g. p. 17 and p. 120.

25. More on that in my essay in *Oecumenica* 1969, p. 22-24.

26. M. Buber has described this "in between" of dialog more than once in an impressive way. Cf. e.g. *Dialogisches Leben,* p. 455 ff. and *Das dialogische Prinzip,* p. 41 and p. 275 f. ("Elemente des Zwischenmenschlichen").

27. The promise of Christ, which is essential for the discovery of truth, "When he comes who is the Spirit of truth, he will guide you into all the truth" (John 16:13, NEB), has played an important role in the evolution of Christian Doctrine, may only be interpreted in terms of dialog.

28. H. Mühlen, *Das Vorverständnis von Person,* Münster, 1965, has characterized the importance of an understanding of the person in ecumenical dialog especially well. Cf. W. Joest, *Die Ontologie der Person bei Luther,* Göttingen, 1967, where this problem is examined in a study of Luther in greater depth.

29. *Das dialogische Prinzip,* p. 32.

30. J. Lacroix, *Le sens du dialogue,* Neuchâtel, 1965, p. 125.

31. V. Vajta, "Theology in Koinonia," in *Lutheran World,* vol. 9, Geneva, 1962, p. 232 ff.

32. As distinct from H. L. Goldschmidt, who always looks at "Dialogik" as a modern form of philosophizing. In M. Buber, "Dialogik" always means the existential relationship to the life of man. The latter concept has the advantage of linking thought based on dialog with life based on dialog. It thus puts it in the context of existence and avoids the danger of an intellectualization.

33. Cf., the dedication of O. Cullmann, *Salvation in History,* London, 1967, p. 6, "... in the faith and hope that even what separates us may contribute to the fluctuating and circuitous progress of salvation history."

34. Cf., the important views on continuity and discontinuity in relation to the unity of the church in K. E. Skydsgaard, "The Hiddenness of God and the Unity of the Church," in *What Unity Implies,* p. 53 ff.

35. Cf., the informative chapter "Having, and Not Having, the Truth," in R. Niebuhr, *The Nature and Destiny of Man,* vol. II, London, 1943, p. 221 ff.

36. H. Küng, *Wahrhaftigkeit,* Freiburg, 1968, rightly repudiates the fanaticism for "truth," citing K. Jaspers, p. 103 ff.

37. K. Rahner, in his essay mentioned above (Note 15), pointed out that the problem of pluralism in theology has more far reaching consequences than the differences between the old schools of thought in theology.

38. Pascal expressly emphasized this view in *Pensées, Oeuvres complètes,* Paris, 1963, p. 592, No. 701, and made it the methodical premise of his "proclamation by dialog" ("De l'art de persuader," *ibid.,* p. 356). On the contribution of Pascal to thinking on dialog, cf. H. Meyer, *Pascals Pensées als dialogische Verkündigung,* Göttingen, 1962, which also indicates the links between Pascal and M. Buber, pp. 32-34.

39. Dialog with atheists, under these conditions, is a task inextricably linked with theology itself. In a discussion in the journal *Esprit,* Paris, 1967, p. 500 ff., this was brought home very strongly in answer to the question whether, viewed from the Christian standpoint, atheism was *"purificateur"* or *"corrupteur."* Cf. also H. Vorgrimler, "Atheism in the View of Recent Catholic Theology," in *Lutheran World,* vol. 13, 1966, p. 26 ff.

40. E. Schillebeeckx speaks, in this context, of an "alien prophecy" ("Fremdprophetie"), *Oecumenica* 1969, p. 176 f., 184. Cf. also J. G. Davies, "The One Witness and the Dialog with the World," *ibid.,* p. 191 f.

41. In a contribution on "The Existence of Man in Dialog" this problem will be dealt with more fully in the second volume under the main title: "The Gospel and the Destiny of Man" by W. Dantine.

42. Kierkegaard, in his diary notes of 1854, looked upon Lutheranism and Protestantism as such "correctives" of Catholicism. But something similar could, no doubt, be said about the relationship of other traditions with each other. Cf. e.g., J.-L. Leuba, "Die Union als ökumenisch-theologisches Problem," in *Um evangelische Einheit,* ed. K. Herbert, Herborn, 1967, pp. 290-324, where the relationship between Lutherans and Reformed is treated from a similar point of view. Somebody might well ask whether the Council of Trent was not, in turn, a Roman corrective for Lutheranism (or the Reformation), which did not escape the danger of going its own way in the course of history. Cf., J. Pelikan, *The Riddle of Roman Catholicism,* New York, 1959, p. 50 ff.

43. In the great change in the Roman Catholic research on Luther as set in motion by the school of J. Lortz, such a "subjective" recognition of Luther is precisely what happened. In the interests of genuine ecumenical dialog, it is Roman Catholics who today demand that Luther and his theological ideas should be taken seriously as a genuine possibility and interest on the part of theology itself. An example of this are the studies of O. H. Pesch, who presents a summary of this complex of problems in an article entitled "Twenty Years of Catholic Luther Research," in *Lutheran World,* vol. 13, 1966, pp. 303-316. Cf. *Wandlungen des Lutherbildes* (Studien und Berichte der Katholischen Akademie in Bayern, Nr. 36), Würzburg, 1966, with special reference to the contribution made by F. W. Kantzenbach and H. Fries. Further, cf. W. Beyna, *Das moderne katholische Lutherbild,* Essen, 1969.

44. This is what happens in M.-J. Le Guillou, *Mission et Unité,* vol. II, Paris, 1960, p. 223 ff., where the author links this with the inevitable development "of a genuine theology of the holy communion." See also Y. Congar, "De fundamento dialogi Ecclesiae cum mundo in natura catholicitatis ad effectum deducendae," in *Acta Congressus Internationalis de Theologia Concilii Vaticani II,* Roma, 1968, pp. 652-661.

45. This tendency is shown in Le Guillou, who identifies the plenitudo catholica with the ecclesiastical reality of the Roman Catholic Church. In a reply to Le Guillou's book mentioned above (Note 44), F. W. Kantzenbach pointed this out: "Communio Sanctorum, Kirche und Konzil," in *Oecumenica* 1966, p. 149 ff.

46. ". . . and in this respect it is not dialectics, but dialog which succeeds in calling evil by its proper name and, patience or no patience, never tolerating, but always fighting it!" (H. L. Goldschmidt in his article mentioned in note 16, p. 200).

47. Teilhard de Chardin, "Panthéisme et Christianisme," in *Comment je crois, Oeuvres*, vol. 10, p. 78.

48. G. Gusdorf, "Dialogue et vérité," in *Oecumenica* 1969, p. 115. Cf. Y. Congar, *Chrétiens en dialogue*, Paris, 1964, p. 17: "Dialog is one of the means by which the diversity of their (i.e., of human beings) perceptions resolve themselves again into a coherent unity towards which everything converges and grows."

49. One cannot warn too strongly against a "materialistic" theology based on a certain intellectual view of the present time, however open-minded we may want to be towards secular theology — or perhaps *because* we want to remain open-minded! The thought that the world can be a threat is fundamental to Holy Scripture, and this is something which most of the advocates of secular theology fail to stress sufficiently. A praiseworthy exception is J. B. Metz, *Zur Theologie der Welt*, Mainz-München, 1968, who warns against that "bad optimism concerning the incarnation, which by virtue of the incarnation of God 'deifies' the world and interprets our salvation as a growing divinisation of the world" (p. 26). The same criticism could, *mutatis mutandis*, be levelled at the divinization of the world by a doctrine of creation, which pictures history without the opposing forces of evil, trying to destroy it, and which pictures the acceptance of the world without the rejection of sin by God. Instead of adducing all sorts of views on this, we shall present this criticism by way of two characteristic statements: "The cosmic God, the God in the mask of the psychologist, and the sociologist hems us in on all sides. So that, when he addresses us he speaks of all but himself, and it only remains for us to turn our backs on him; in order to meet — perhaps — God." (J.-L. Nancy, "Catéchisme de persévérance," in *Esprit* No. 10, 1967, p. 376.) And: "If the world draws away from God, from the church, it is because all that the church — we — offers is merely human — and this often secondhand" (Y. Pellé-Douel in the Enquête of the journal *Esprit, ibid.*, p. 436).

50. J. Aagaard, "Witness and Dialog in Missionary Perspective," in *Oecumenica* 1969, p. 132 aptly differentiates between inter-humanistic, inter-religious, inter-covenantal, and inter-confessional dialog. T. de Chardin in one place speaks of the necessary distinction between an "ecumenism from the basis" and an "ecumenism at the top" ("Oecuménisme," in *Oeuvres*, vol. 9, Paris, 1965, p. 253 f.)

51. Foreword by J.-M. Domenach to the special edition about Nouveau monde et parole de Dieu, *Esprit* No. 10, 1967, p. 357.

Chapter 2

Ecumenical Endeavor and Its Quest for Motivation

THE PROBLEM OF MOTIVATION TODAY

Today the question of the motive or motives of our ecumenical work has again become very acute. This fundamental question of the "why" and the "wherefore" of church unity underlies all the discussions of the form of the church unity being sought, of ecumenical methods, of particular factors and problems which divide churches, and of possible forms of cooperation. Thus it appears that also in ecumenical thought we must return to the basic principles.

In a 1964 address figuring up the "bank balance" after a half century of ecumenical activity, Visser 't Hooft said:

> We are still suffering from an uncertainty as to the motivation of the ecumenical movement. The inner strength and true dynamic of a movement depend primarily on the clarity and purity of its motivation and secondarily on the forthrightness with which the decisive motive is advanced and defended.[1]

Four years later, in his address to the plenary assembly in Uppsala on "The Mandate of the Ecumenical Movement," Visser 't Hooft once again took up the question of motivation in his attempt to bridge the gap between ecumenical "verticalists" and "horizontalists."

The discussions which have taken place during this time have brought to light both this uncertainty of motivation and the central significance of the motive question. The noticeable shifts in the way Christian unity is understood from — to use labels — a church-oriented ecumenism to a world-oriented ecumenism, shifts which have been described as a change in the substance of the ecumenical movement,[2] must first and foremost be understood as a profound change of motive.

It is not really surprising that these shifts are now taking place; on the contrary, it is a natural and necessary process. The work of ecumenism is presently being passed on from one generation to another. As part of this transfer, the basic understanding and pre-suppositions of this work must be re-examined critically. Only in this way can a true transfer and appropriation by the new generation come about.

But now it is everywhere apparent that in this present transition there is an unusually large amount of criticism of traditional ecumenical thought and action. The catch-word, "the post-ecumenical age," perhaps makes this clearer than anything else, for in it there is expressed something almost like a rejection of ecumenism or at least a refusal to be identified any longer with the ecumenical movement in its past form.

At what is this criticism directed?

It has often been said that the slow progress in ecclesiastical efforts at unity, their getting bogged down in talk, and the lack of responsible steps and decisions are to blame for this. Certainly that is correct. But this criticism is not anything new today. The ecumenical movement realized it was confronted with the problem of credibility very soon after its beginning. This problem was addressed repeatedly, often by speaking of the "impatience of youth," which wanted to see declarations of unity cashed into binding decisions.

On the surface, it appears as though this gap between procla-mations of unity and their realization is felt more acutely today than ever. Nevertheless, it is clear that the present criticism of the ecumenical movement's traditional form strikes still deeper. It is directed at the basic orientation of ecumenical thought and action. Efforts for church unity, it is said, have become a preoccupation of the church with itself and as such are irrelevant. So the thing to do now is to "get down to business" and to understand efforts for church unity (if they are not to be questioned altogether) clearly and consistently from the perspective of the church's mission in our world and to orient those efforts toward that mission. Thus this criticism poses the question of motive, that which gives our efforts for unity the right impetus and the right orientation.

THE PLURALITY OF MOTIVES AND THE CENTRALITY OF THE THEOLOGICAL-ECCLESIOLOGICAL MOTIVE

How could this criticism have arisen? Is it based on something in the origin and development of the ecumenical movement? Some, especially the historically well-informed, will quickly answer no to this question and will have no difficulty in marshalling up good reasons for their answer. Simply referring to the origin of the modern ecumenical movement in the World Missionary Conference in Edinburgh (1910) shows how central and constitutive the motive of mission has been and how from the very beginning everything seems to point outward, away from a preoccupation of the church with itself. For this reason, Catholic observers like M.-J. Le Guillou, for example, have understood the ecumenical movement as the "outgrowth of a missionary movement." Of the World Council he writes: "It is simply a brotherhood of churches in which everything is oriented toward evangelizing the world and testifying to Christ's royal reign. It intends to be a search for fellowship for the sake of mission." [3]

Now it is widely recognized that in the origin and development of the ecumenical movement, many other motives besides the mission-evangelization motive were at work: especially the social-ethical motive, the desire in the face of the modern social and political problems to lead the churches to practical cooperation in the spirit of the Christian ethic, and the theological-ecclesiological motive, the desire to express the God-given essential unity of the church in faith, order, and worship. The embodiments of these two motives in, respectively, the movements for Life and Work and Faith and Order are closely related in content and history to the mission-evangelization motive; and yet each one of these three

demonstrates a clear independence. The parallels and many inter-
sections between all three movements made their unification in
the World Council of Churches (WCC) possible. Also the relative
independence of the motives standing behind each movement
caused an inner tension and consequently a struggle within the
WCC over their proper coordination and priority.

Can it be said that any one of these main motives has gained
predominance in the course of the development of the ecumenical
movement? The present uncertainty in the question of motivation,
referred to in the above quotation from Visser 't Hooft, makes it
clear that this question is not easy to answer. This is due primarily
to the fact that within the WCC there are various relatively independent areas of responsibility and work, which correspond to
these different motives. This is in accord with the WCC's mandate,
which consists of, among other things, "to carry on the work of
the world movements for Faith and Order, Life and Work, and of
the International Missionary Council." Thus the preservation of
each of the original motives and the refusal to give up any of
them is anchored in the constitution of the WCC. This in turn is
reflected in the assemblies, especially in the topics and work of
the various sections. In addition, all the motives appear to have
become so tightly woven together that it is no longer possible to
separate them clearly. Just as the one or the other surface of a
diamond flashes according to the angle from which it is viewed,
so also in the question of the dominant ecumenical motive, the
one or the other motive becomes prominent according to the
position from which the question is approached.

Then is the question of the dominant motive perhaps forced or
improper? Should it not be posed at all?

The question is historically and materially inescapable. As Visser
't Hooft rightly said, "the inner strength and the true dynamic"
of the ecumenical movement depend directly on a clear and unambiguous motivation. Therefore the question of which of the
conflicting motives is the decisive one has been posed again and
again, and again and again attempts have been made to answer it.

Despite everything that must be said about the importance and
influence of other motives, we certainly are not wrong in seeing
the pathos and the distinguishing characteristic of the ecumenical

movement, especially in its second phase, beginning with the conferences of 1937, in the repeated establishment and retention of the theological-ecclesiological motive, often even in polemical form, as the basic sustaining motive. The unity of the church, as the New Testament and the ancient church creeds confess it, belongs to the God-ordained essence of the church; division of the church is contrary to God's will and to the essential unity of the church; therefore our efforts for unity are obedience to God's will for unity and have their goal in making the essential unity of the church visible in confession, worship, and the office of the ministry.

The central significance of the theological-ecclesiological motive becomes increasingly evident in the various stages and documents of the ecumenical movement. It is expressed, for example, in the "God wills fellowship" of the first sentence of the 1920 Lambeth Conference's "Appeal to All Christian People," or the first sentence of the "Call to Unity" of the first World Conference for Faith and Order (1927). It is articulated in that rather "basic principle" of ecumenism which crystallized very early: that the oneness of the church is a previously given gift of God and therefore the ecumenical task must be understood as to manifest, to realize in history, or to incarnate this given oneness — in short, that the ecumenical imperative must be based on the ecumenical indicative. Finally, the central significance of the theological-ecclesiological motive is also evident in the special importance given from the very beginning within the WCC to the work of the Commission on Faith and Order in the treatment of the unity question and in the so-called "St. Andrew Formula" (1960), worked out by that commission, accepted by the central committee, and presented before the assembly in New Delhi; in this formula the WCC tried, for the first and as yet only time, to define its understanding of the unity of the church.

How the central significance of this theological-ecclesiological motive was advocated, defended, and retained can be seen very clearly from Visser 't Hooft's essays and addresses, which cover a period of more than three decades. What is present already in his first address from 1935 on "Confessing the One Holy Christian Church" and from then on at every step of the way is entirely consistent with what he writes toward the end of his activity as

General Secretary of the WCC when figuring the "bank balance" of the ecumenical movement:

> There is only one motive which can give the (ecumenical) movement real power and independence, namely the fact that fellowship belongs to the essence of the church itself and that every form of division obscures God's plan for his people. . . . The church needs fellowship not because it is useful, desirable, or pleasant, but because fellowship belongs to the essence of its life.

Therefore, faced with the variety of motives, it is important "to concentrate on this one, decisive, and fully sufficient motive." [4]

It is not only the WCC's understanding of unity which has been marked by the predominance of the theological-ecclesiological motive. Despite different forms and applications, it also marks the understanding of unity and of ecumenical obligation held for many years in the various individual churches and confessional groupings. That is clearly true of the Orthodox church and its understanding of unity oriented around the concept of the "ancient undivided church." [5] It applies likewise to the Roman Catholic understanding of unity as expressed in the *Decree on Ecumenism.*[6] The Lutheran understanding of unity can also be referred to. Here, too, the starting point is the given oneness of the church of Christ: "Men reconciled to God are one in Jesus Christ." Therefore ecumenical efforts are aimed at "manifesting the unity of the Church in visible church fellowship." [7] Thus the indicative automatically produces the imperative.

All of this answers the *quaestio facti* and shows how much the theological-ecclesiological motive was and to a great extent still is the point of departure and orientation of efforts for Christian unity. Because present-day criticism starts out from this view of the facts, it must be granted validity; it cannot be intercepted at this point — for instance by referring to other equally influential contributing motives.

Why was this motive placed in the center as the decisive motive?

In the last analysis, it was to show that the issue of the church's unity is not simply a question that can be weighed and discussed or something which may be more or less profitable or useful, but rather something which is essential and absolutely necessary for the church. It is not external pressures, for example from the state, the threat of atheistic systems, advancing secularization, or the attack of nonChristian ideologies, that give rise to the call to unity. Nor do the currents of the spirit of the times (ideas of tolerance) or socio-political developments (growing interdependence between peoples, international federations, etc.) give rise to it. The true motive for unity also does not lie in practical considerations such as, for example, the fact that the division of the churches means a dissipation of their resources in mission work and social ministry, makes it more difficult to hear the Christian message and detracts from the credibility of the Christian witness. Each of these motives is thoroughly justifiable. They are not wrong, but they become wrong as soon as they — or one of them — are viewed as sufficient motivation. For then Christian unity is something peripheral, some-thing "debatable"; then the ecumenical movement has "no real life, no real business of its own." [8]

Therefore everything depends on recognizing the theological, christological, and biblical foundation of unity and of the attempts to achieve unity as well as on establishing the ecumenical impera-tive in the indicative: in the reality of the one Lord and head of the church and in the oneness of the church which is thus given, as the Holy Scripture testifies. Then "there can be no real debate over the necessity of full fellowship"; then we no longer think of the unity of the church "moralistically," but rather "theologically"; [9] then we have really come "to the point" in our question of unity, *i.e.*, we pose the question of the church's unity in such a way that it "is identical with the question of Jesus Christ as the real head and Lord of the church." [10]

> We must be one for this reason and for this reason alone, because only in this way do we all have a share in the one work of God. It is not that we serve God better, or help one another better, or give the world a clearer witness when we are one. Rather it is that we serve God at all only then, that we help one another at all only then, that we give the world a faithful witness at all only then, when we are about God's work and not preoccupied with ourselves, when all together we submit ourselves to God's work and are one in it. There is only one church, and everything that keeps this church from ex-

pressing its essential unity is therefore the work of man and is sin.[11]

THE PROBLEM OF INCORPORATING THE COMMISSION MOTIVE INTO THE THEOLOGICAL-ECCLESIOLOGICAL MOTIVE

This quotation leads on to the question how the central theological-ecclesiological motive is related to what can be called the "commission motive" (comprising both the mission-evangelization motive and the socio-ethical motive) for ecumenical efforts.

There can be no talk of isolating the commission motive and of setting it aside as of no consequence next to the theological-ecclesiological motive. The WCC Central Committee's oft-quoted declaration of 1951 ("The Calling of the Church to Mission and Unity") makes that very evident. It has been emphasized repeatedly that the unity of the church is not an end in itself, that it is sought "not for its own sake." [12] Therefore almost everywhere where the theological-ecclesiological motive is formulated and set forth there is, usually in the immediate context, also a reference to the church's commission in the world in witness and ministry.[13] Visser 't Hooft has rightly seen this as one of the main points in the unity question on which there is agreement within the WCC: "Unity must be sought not for its own sake, but rather for the sake of the world in which the church has the task of missionary proclamation." [14] But in defining the relationship between the theological-ecclesiological motive on the one hand and the commission motive on the other hand, we must go still a step further: rightly understood, here the ecumenical imperative to express the already-given unity is viewed as one and the same thing as the church's commission; for all the concepts which occur in this context, such as "manifest," "make visible," "cause to appear," etc., have their point of reference *not* in the church or the believers, but rather in the world. What is necessary is to make the given unity, of which faith is already certain, visible in and before the world and in this way to testify to God's unifying and reconciling work. Thus to establish the theological-ecclesiological motive as the decisive and sufficient motive does not mean to exclude the commission motive. It also does not mean first isolating the idea of commission from the idea of unity in order then, in a second step, to bring it back in again. In reality — and this is typical — one does not even differentiate between the realization of visible unity and commission. Both are one and the same: making its unity visible is in itself the church's commission to the world. For this visible unity is witness. It is, as it were, the epiphany to the world of God's reconciling and unifying work in Christ. "The given unity which must be revealed . . . is the manifestation of the activity of the great Shepherd. The church which has been gathered together owes the masses who have no shepherd clear evidence that the shepherd really is about his business." [15]

This is the real intention behind setting forth the theological-ecclesiological motive. Anything which might appear to depreciate the commission motive is in reality an argument against separating or even differentiating between unity and commission; it is an attempt to see them both as one and the same thing and to understand unity as commission. The Johannine saying: ". . . that they also may be one in us, so that the world may believe" (17:21), is in full accord with this view; it makes a direct connection between the disciples' unity and the world's coming to faith, without any link in the chain of logic — for instance a reference to the disciples' missionary activity or their joint witness.

Perhaps to some it could appear as a petty difference, whether we now say: attaining visible unity in itself is the church's commission to the world, or whether we say: the church's unity serves the church's commission by helping to make the Christian proclamation clearer, richer, more convincing, and giving the church's diaconic and social action greater comprehensiveness and scope. Do not both formulations concentrate on the commission for which the church lives? Do not both views make it clear that church unity is not sought as an end in itself and that our ecumenical efforts are not an introverted preoccupation of the church itself?

Despite their similarity, the difference between these two views cannot be minimized. For one, as has already been shown, this difference has been maintained repeatedly in the past; secondly, it is precisely here that the root of the present disagreement lies and it is, in the last analysis, from this point of view that the clear present-day shift in the way ecumenical commitment is being understood will have to be evaluated and judged. For the under-standing of commission and of unity takes on an entirely different color, according to whether one holds the one or the other of these views of their relationship.

If the visible unity of the church in itself is mission, witness, and service, and if the idea of commission is drawn up completely into the idea of unity, then the character of commission is to dem-onstrate redemption and reconciliation to the world. The church's commission in the world then is to designate itself as a sign of the reality of reconciliaton — a sign which is in the world, but never-theless is erected over against the world, a sign which the world is sure to be able to perceive, understand, and accept. Consequently, every concern for the proper realization of the commission concen-trates on this sign itself; it must reflect that reality to which it is supposed to point fully and without distortion. Therefore the concern about how this sign and the reality it points to can reach and penetrate the world, be understood and accepted by it and be effective in it is, in the last analysis, resolved in the certainty that the sign is self-evident and that the reality to which it points is effective in itself.

The church's mission appears in quite a different light when the visible unity of the church in itself is not granted this quality of witness, when the commission idea is thus not incorporated into the unity idea but rather the unity of the church is functionally or instrumentally coordinated with or subordinated to the church's witness and service. Here the accent clearly shifts to the question of how the church's testimony to and service of reconciliation can reach the world and be accepted by it as answer and help. But one cannot pose this question, to say nothing of answering it, unless he first experiences just what the world's questions and needs are. Thus the service of reconciliation commissioned to the church is essentially more than to point to and manifest to the world the reality of reconciliation. The service of reconciliation is first and foremost the concern that reconciliation happens in the world. From this point of view church unity and efforts for unity are to be understood. If the disunity of the churches is more than a dis-unity between each other and more than just a failure to manifest reconciled reality but is rather a real contradiction as to what the church has to do and to say as the servant of reconciliation in the world, and if the divisions of the church not only prevent it from making its God-given unity visible but rather for their own part even create and deepen divisions between men and peoples, then church unity is not primarily a sign but rather an instrument, not primarily a manifestation but rather a factor, of reconciliation.

It is easy to burden each of these different ways of understanding and relating the church's unity and mission with depreciating labels. That should be avoided, since it would certainly mean dealing in caricatures, and that means polemics and abstractions. But the question of what is right or wrong here can hardly be answered polemically and in abstracto. Which view appears as "right" and therefore moves into the foreground will depend to a great extent on the historical situation in which the church is living. For example, it must be taken into account whether the social and political situation in which a church is living makes room for missionary and social involvement or prevents or restricts it. Consequently, the church will then understand and carry out its commission and its commitment to unity with emphasis either on a world-oriented and world-penetrating activity or on a more passive manifestation.

A look into the New Testament especially should make us cautious about any attempt to pose these alternatives in this question too hastily. Even if the historical difference between the New Testament and the present-day situation is taken fully into account, with all that that includes precisely as regards the unity question, it is nevertheless possible to find something like New Testament counterparts for both of these views.

On the one side, for example, Paul could be referred to — especially his use of the "body of Christ" concept, which in fact is one of the key ideas for ecumenical thought. More recent exegesis has — although not without opposition — attempted to show that Paul uses this concept, contrary to the history of religions background, to say something not about the "essence" but rather about the "function" of the church. [16] The congregation, as the body of Christ, is the place in which Christ "wants to get out into the world," "seeks and serves the world" through the members of his body.[17] In its entirety and in the united efforts of its members — the "instruments of his grace" — it is the locale "of this grace, which is constantly spreading out over everything and which, in the abundance of its spiritual gifts, leaves no time and no place without its promise and its demand." [18]

This Pauline view, which sees the church in its entirety and in its unity oriented towards the world in a dynamic relationship of seeking and serving, could be contrasted with a Johannine view. This Johannine understanding must admittedly be seen against the broader horizon of a new phase in the development of early Christian history; therefore it is reflected partially in modified form also in other parts of the New Testament. Here unity is above all an essential mark of the church, based on the heavenly unity of the Father with the Son and the Son with the Father. It can

> be testified to as the earthly mark of the Christian congregation only for this reason . . . , because it was pre-figured in the relationship of the Father and the Son and because it has been transferred to the earthly community through the work of both the Father and the Son.[19]

Closely related to this view is the concept of a more strongly dualistic relationship between church and world, featuring a clear opposition between the two. True, the sending of the church into the world is emphasized very much (John 17:18), but "not even in the consciousness of its sending does the church feel any solidarity with the secular." [20] The goal of mission is to gather the scattered children of God through the Word (John 11:52). This word, as a word pronounced by Jesus, is his self-manifestation as revealer and retains this proclamatory and revelatory nature also in the mouths of the disciples. The disciples' unity, granted in answer to Jesus' prayer, participates in this self-revelation of Jesus. It is the reflection of the unity between the Father and the Son and it lets the world recognize that the Son has been sent from the Father (John 17:23; cf. 17:21).

THE NEW DEFINITION OF THE CENTRAL MOTIVE

To ask abstractly which of these two views of unity and mission is right or wrong, as though it were a matter of free choice between two alternatives, is a questionable procedure also because the answer is always co-determined by the intellectual environment in which each of the churches is living. Thus the rise to predominance of the theological-ecclesiological motive toward the end of the thirties can hardly be understood without taking into account the changes in the theological "climate" taking place at that time: the rise of recent biblical theology, the rediscovery of the church as an integrating element of the Christian message, and the lasting influence of dialectical theology.

Today there is another new change in the general intellectual environment. This change is expressed in the shift of ecclesiological and theological interest — to use generalizing labels — from dialectic to dialog, from identity to solidarity, from manifestation to participation. This change is evident especially in the church's new consciousness of solidarity with the world and its problems and in the demand for the church's active participation in the social, economic, technical, and political revolutions of our time. It is evident — on the negative side — in a clear neglect of the ecclesiological interest, of church and denominational self-consciousness, and in a criticism of the church's outward institutional forms and traditional structures. Although it is expressed in varying degrees of intensity, this criticism is universal, and in most of it there can be heard undertones of the basic question: how much does the church need fixed structures and institutional elements at all in order to carry out its commission? Finally, this change in the general theological atmosphere today can also be seen in the new radical way of understanding the missionary task: the diaspora and missionary situation of the church on every continent is not only taken seriously, but is even affirmed as the natural situation of the church. This new way of understanding mission opposes any attempt once again to see the goal of mission as "plantatio ecclesiae," that is to gather the church together, instead of understanding the church as leaven in the world.

Inevitably, these changes have had a direct influence on ecumenical thought. In the course of these changes, the theological-ecclesiological motive for unity, in a certain sense automatically and only secondarily as the result of purposeful debate, began to lose the predominant position it had had and its motivating power.

The time has long since passed in which this changed way of thinking and the resulting new definition of the ecumenical task was restricted to avant-garde groups and their representatives, although it was there that it developed both its polemical sharpness and simultaneously its one-sidedness. It is becoming increasingly evident how the churches in toto are being drawn into this change. This fact must be given full consideration. It shows to what extent the material integration of "ecclesiastical" and "secular" ecumenism has already begun and how already now the recently emphasized antithesis between these two forms of ecumenical thought and action is being shown to be illusory — in spite of the reluctance of certain groups to be integrated.

A comparative analysis of three positions on the unity question taken within the past two years in the WCC, the Anglican Communion, and the Lutheran World Federation can elucidate that. Under consideration are — in chronological order — the report of section I at Uppsala ("The Holy Spirit and the Catholicity of the Church"), the report of section II of the last Lambeth Conference ("Renewal of the Church in Unity"),[21] and the study document of the Lutheran World Federation's Commission on Theology ("More than Church Unity").[22] Only a sketchy and simplified comparison of these three texts can be drawn here; the material differences which exist between and even within the individual positions, important as they are, are not made explicit. But they do have four basic things in common, which to some extent reflect very plainly the changes in ecumenical thought.

1. Neither Christ's founding action nor the church's essential oneness and actual divisions is the real point of departure in the quest for church unity. The world and humanity in their disruption and tensions, as well as in their suffering and seeking for unity and reconciliation are the point of departure. This point of departure is chosen consciously and to some extent — as for example in the report of the Lambeth Conference — is explicitly differentiated from a traditional understanding of unity which begins with the church: "We approach our subject with a changed perspective. We find ourselves impelled — but gladly impelled — to think first of the world. Its divisions clamour for healing and we see God's pur-

pose for its unity as a cause even more urgent than the unity of the church." Thus, as it is expressed for example in the programmatic title of the Lutheran study document, what is at stake from the very start is more than just *church* division and *church* unity.

This does not at all mean that now the subject is approached un-theologically. On the contrary! This new point of departure is understood and established theologically — although there are clear and not inconsiderable differences in the way this is done. One view sees the world as the sphere of God's continuous activity as creator and making the world whole as the final goal of the Christ event and the Christian message. Another view considers the world in itself as the place in which the Holy Spirit is at work making things new and whole everywhere — even out beyond the Christian proclamation, faith in Christ and the church. But all the various views have this one thing in common: they understand and establish the new starting point of the ecumenical question theologically in a way intended to obviate from the beginning any ecclesiological narrowing of ecumenical activity.

2. This orientation toward the unity and reconciliation of the world, which now marks the whole approach to the question of ecumenism, is no longer described in predominantly cognitive categories. Where there was a primarily theological-ecclesiological understanding of unity it was commonly said that the church's commission is, in its own unity, to manifest, express, and let the world recognize God's reconciling work; such expressions no longer do justice to this new orientation of ecumenical thought and endeavor, but rather are more apt to obscure it again.

The relationship between the unity and reconcilation of the churches and the unity and reconciliation of the world is now seen as a relationship of service. This means that the church, in its efforts for unity, not only manifests reconciled reality to the world but even actively participates in God's reconciling and unifying work on and in the world. Therefore the tendency to speak of the church as the "image" or "sign" of reconciled reality is being superseded and surpassed by descriptions of the church as the "tool," the "instrument," the "effective sign" of reconciliation. In keeping with this, the church's relationship to the world is described chiefly in terms of work, effectiveness, and help. In its efforts for unity, the church must carry on Christ's reconciling work in the world, bringing enemies together, liberating the oppressed, overcoming racial barriers, healing social and political divisions, and bridging the gap between rich and poor. In all this the "dynamization" of the understanding of unity is evident. Where traditional cognitive concepts are still used, they are often used or interpreted in a new more "dynamic" sense. The way in which the church's attributes according to the Uppsala report — especially apostolicity and catholicity — are transformed or at least broadened from distinguishing marks and essential characteristics into directions for a world-oriented service and descriptions of functions is typical of this "dynamization."

3. Emphasizing the ideas of service and commission by no means bypasses or pushes aside the question of the church's unity. On the contrary, the quest for church unity is an integrating factor in this world-oriented and world-penetrating service of reconciliation and unification. This is already obvious to the extent that divisions between the church for their own part cause and deepen social tensions and conflict so that to overcome these ecclesiastical divisions *ipso facto* has an effect in the social sphere. Primarily, however, church unity is a question of the church's usefulness as an instrument of reconciliation. A witness to Christ as the one reconciler which — in all its necessary diversity — lacks concord and which therefore cannot be given by all the churches jointly is a profound self-contradiction which robs that witness of its missionary power and outreach. A witness which isolates itself and is intent on marking itself off from other forms of the Christian witness also stands in danger of narrowing and impoverishing that witness. The same is true of diaconic and social action; divisions in the church detract from its unity of mission and weaken its effect. For that reason the report of the Lambeth Conference declares: "Unity is desirable . . . in order that the church may be a better tool than at present in the service of God's purpose for the world." [24]

Thereby instead of letting the commission motive be absorbed in the theological-ecclesiological motive, now the theological-ecclesiological motive is coordinated with and subordinated to the com-

mission motive; thus church unity is understood as a fellowship
in the service of reconciliation. One of the last sections of the
Lutheran study document, recapitulating the document's whole
chain of thought, reflects this in every sentence:

> Our theological endeavor for consensus in understanding the
> gospel serves the purpose of reaching all mankind with the
> liberating and consoling message of the one savior. The over-
> coming of church divisions and breaking through denomina-
> tional isolation gives greater scope and effectiveness to the
> diaconic and social engagement of Christians. The surrender
> of confessional complacency and the respect for the convic-
> tions of others helps to diminish the explosiveness of human
> and social conflicts. The struggle for fellowship among all
> Christians, in which social and cultural differences, race mem-
> bership, and national ties have lost their divisive power, is
> part of the great battle for the healing of a world lacerated
> by tension and enmity.[25]

Thus there is now something like a "pragmatization" of the
understanding of unity (i.e., the return to prominence of the long-
neglected question of the usefulness and relevance of church unity
for the church's actual service in the world); it corresponds to the
"dynamization" of the understanding of unity. This question of
usefulness has also become a criterion for judging church unity
and efforts for unity, so that "obedience to the commission may
oblige us to reject a unity which does not serve these objectives"
(*sc.* common witness and unity of mankind).[26]

4. It would be a misunderstanding to say that orienting efforts
for unity to the world's needs and conflicts limits the church's
commission of reconciliation to the area of diaconic and social
action. This new orientation does not imply that at all. The service
of reconciliation commissioned to the church always includes both:
reconciliation of men with God and with each other. In this sense
"witness," or "mission," and "service" are kept together as two
dimensions of the one and the same commission of reconciliation.
That is clearly evident in the fact that the final goal of all Christian
efforts for unity, the unity of all men, is always understood as
"mankind renewed in Christ," as "to guide mankind to a common

praise of God," as the reconciliation of all men "in the one divine sonship of which Christ is both the author and finisher." [27]

There is no attempt to define the relationship of "witness" and "service" by describing their order of importance; that would place into doubt the fact that essentially they belong together. But it remains clear that — for Christians — it is reconciliation with God, graciously given in Word and Sacrament, which liberates them and calls them to the service of reconciliation among men. Therefore church unity has a profound spiritual and worship dimension, even and indeed precisely when it is understood as a fellowship in the service of reconciliation in the world or in the sense of "dynamic catholicity." Its "constitutive center . . . is corporate worship in which Christ himself is the one who both calls and sends." [28] Thus the new orientation of the understanding of unity does not bypass the question of joint worship and all the individual questions tied to it (the understanding of the sacrament, liturgical confessions, the office of the ministry). However, perhaps more so than formerly, it places these questions under the aspect of commission, in as much as the endeavor for church unity as a fellowship in the service of reconciliation in the world simply cannot ignore the fact that the gift and the commission of reconciliation are received by all of us together, and not separately and in different ways.

CONSEQUENCES FOR ECUMENICAL THOUGHT AND ACTION

The process of redefining the central motive for unity is certainly not yet finished. Reaction and triteness, radicalization and over-exaggeration are all still very possible developments. In the present situation it appears important to reflect on the implications and consequences of this new definition for future ecumenical endeavors. The following is an attempt to do that on several points.

The Quest for Diversity

Orienting ecumenical thought and action more strongly toward the church's commission in the world strengthens and deepens the insight into the necessity of diversity in the Christian service; for the many-faceted world can be penetrated only by a many-faceted ministry.

Certainly the insistence that church unity does not mean uniformity is as old as the ecumenical movement itself. It was, however, applied mostly to the narrower areas of church government and organization.[29] Things were different with regard to the variety and diversity in witness, doctrine, the office of the ministry, and worship. Here there was a phase which tended to tolerate uncritically this diversity or even to extol it as the expression of the richness of Christianity as a whole; this was followed by a basically critical phase. True, it was recognized that the historical rise of the various Christian traditions was, at least partially, justified and that therefore these differences must be examined in mutual respect. There was even talk of the "good diversity," which reflected the variety of the gifts of the spirit and of creation, and it was seen how already the New Testament itself contains diverse forms of expression of the one faith in Christ. The attempt — roughly since New Delhi — to interpret the concept of "unity" with the concept of "fellowship" *(koinonia)* must also be understood as, among other things, a denial of the idea of uniformity and support for "lively variety" in the body of Christ. Nevertheless, the diversity of Christian traditions was felt to be, in the last analysis, an embarrassing diversity, a potential cause of division which must be overcome if one really wishes to get beyond a mere cooperation and achieve the unity of the churches.[30] The desire to do this led to attempts to set forth the common center of these traditions, to seek their reciprocal supplementation and correction, to emphasize their temporary nature in the face of the judgment of the returning Christ, or to examine them in joint study of Scripture and to renew them in common obedience to Christ.

These two attitudes, uncritical affirmation and critical questioning of variety and diversity, are similar in that they consider and judge variety and diversity primarily in their existing historical forms. But this is a narrow view of the problem. It poses the question in one of only two alternatives: whether viewed historically, the rise of the diversity was justified, or whether what has come down from history is valid or invalid in the present-day situation. But the full breadth of this problem is really grasped only when it is realized that the question of the variety and diversity does not arise merely in the form of the diversity of historical traditions, but rather arises constantly and inevitably in the process of handing on the gospel.

This basic historical nature of the proclamation and understanding of the gospel appears to have been clearly seen, recognized in its essential connection with the church's missionary commission and included in the understanding of unity for the first time — in the ecumenical movement — at the Fourth World Conference for Faith and Order in Montreal (1963).

> We have recognized . . . that tradition looks also to the present and to the future. The church is sent by Christ to proclaim the Gospel to all men; the tradition must be handed on in time and also in space. In other words, tradition has a vital missionary dimension in every land, for the command of the Lord is to go to all nations.[31]

Then, in the course of establishing the commission motive, this new estimation of diversity was made explicit in Uppsala. Under the very significant title "The Quest for Diversity," it says in the report of Section I: "Diversity may be a perversion of catholicity but often it is a genuine expression of the apostolic vocation of the church. . . . By such diversities . . . the Spirit leads us forward on the way to a fully catholic mission and ministry." [32]

Therefore, in the quest for church unity as a fellowship in the service of reconciliation in the world, the real concern can no longer be to abolish differences. Also, there can no longer be a biased concern to interpret and maintain traditional differences as a justified, perhaps even a complementary diversity. Above all else, there must be a search and a demand for the diversity necessary for today's witness and service.

That means that in the quest for the legitimate diversity the beginning point can no longer be primarily the historically shaped existing differences, be they of a confessional or a geographical nature. How the differences shaped in the past can be understood as a legitimate variety is, for all its importance, first a historical problem. The answer to it still does not solve the question of church unity as a fellowship in the service of reconciliation in the world. The crucial question is the question of the new diversity demanded by today. Certainly it also includes the search for renewal and *Aggiornamento* of the traditional diversity, but it does not end there; it goes beyond that. The phenomenon, evident for some time now, "that the old confessional divisions are being crisscrossed by new lines of agreement and disagreement" because "many of the most pressing and troubling problems of the modern world have arisen subsequent to the forming of our separate traditions," [33] makes clear what is involved. It also shows how this process of the rise of a new diversity is already under way and cannot be fit into the old efforts for merging already-formed traditions.

The question of the traditional diversity can be rightly posed only in the perspective of this search for the new diversity demanded by today. For the new diversity cannot be found in a responsible manner without taking seriously into account the traditional diversity. The problem is to what extent this traditional diversity still has its functional value today, so that it must be considered necessary for the church's present-day service. This puts the question to each different tradition and to the identities which constitute them: are they ready to lay themselves open to a thorough transformation, a new definition of their identity in answer to the present-day demands for the service of reconciliation in the world?

Cooperation and Consensus

Orienting ecumenical thought and action more strongly toward the church's commission implies a new estimation and a new understanding of Christian and church cooperation. Instead of such cooperation being viewed as merely a preliminary stage and a means to church unity, joint action in the world in witness and service must be understood as the goal of ecumenical endeavor and a touchstone of church unity.

This estimation of cooperation is anything but a new insight. Like the emphasis on the commission motive, with which it goes hand in hand, it leads back to the beginnings of the ecumenical movement. As is well known, the idea of the churches' cooperation and joint practical action stood right in the center at the World

Missionary Conference in Edinburgh (1910) and the founding of the International Missionary Council (1921), as well as in the encyclical of the Ecumenical Patriarchate (1920), and the Life and Work movement — to name only a few determinative events and movements.

This interest in cooperation — at least in the beginning — was marked by the conviction that all Christians could work together without regarding the question of theological and ecclesiological disagreement or consensus. It was not, they said, the theological consensus but rather the tasks and problems which confronted all churches and Christians together and whose extraordinary urgency they all felt together that made joint action possible. This conviction was even reinforced by their perception of the problems confronting them as *new* problems, which demonstrated no direct link to traditional church-divisive differences. Everywhere — in the area of mission work as well as in the area of social responsibility — there was the feeling of being confronted with the specific "urgent needs of the present," a "new world," a "new age," and "new task," determined by new national, economic, social, or political convulsions and developments (Message of the Edinburgh World Missionary Conference). Thus also in face of the shape of the tasks to be accomplished, renunciation of theological and ecclesiological consensus and concentration on "united practical action" (Message of the Stockholm World Conference of Churches) appeared to be the necessary path.

Inspired by this kind of ecumenical thought and yet also critically removing itself from it, there arose a new way of understanding unity and a new form of the ecumenical movement; from the very beginning on it held up "organic unity" as the "ideal which all Christians should have in their thoughts and prayers." [34] Now the question of consensus and fellowship in faith and order, which had at first been set aside, was placed with great emphasis in the center of interest, while on the other hand the question of cooperation was pushed off to the periphery. It was clear already at the first World Conference for Faith and Order (1927) that in the larger context of this understanding of unity, cooperation in missionary work and in the social sphere had at the very most only a propaedeutic function for ecumenism. Cooperation was understood as a matter of "comity, mutual consideration, and Christian courtesy" and to that extent as a "way of approach." But the real goal, full church fellowship in faith, sacrament, and office of the ministry, lay beyond all cooperation.[35]

In saying this, the Faith and Order movement — as strange as it may seem — succumbed to basically the same error as, for instance, the World Missionary Conference of Edinburgh or the early Life and Work movement. Quite apart from the fully different position assigned to joint practical action in such case, there was agreement on the basic idea that cooperation of the churches in missionary work, in the social sphere, in questions of education, etc., was possible even when theological and ecclesiological questions were largely disregarded.

Now it is of interest and of great consequence for the further development of ecumenical thought that this error was seen and corrected very quickly within the Life and Work movement, while it kept itself alive within the Faith and Order movement.

The concept of a cooperation between the churches which ignores theological and ecclesiological questions proved to be an illusion already at the first World Conference for Life and Work. True, the letter of invitation and even still the concluding report spoke of the desire of "leaving for the time our differences in faith and order" and limiting ourselves entirely to "common action on the part of all Christians." [36] However, deep differences of opinion arose, especially in the conception of the kingdom of God, in which confessional-theological factors played in to a great extent; these showed that questions of faith and church unity cannot be set aside even in efforts for joint practical action by all Christians.

The Life and Work movement drew the logical conclusions. It recognized more and more the importance of the question of the church and its essential nature and affirmed the search for theological consensus — in the broad sense — as that which gives Christians' social action both the right orientation and thereby also the quality of joint action. The study conferences which followed the Stockholm Conference, and especially the second World Conference of Churches in Oxford (1937), showed how the question of joint action was now being dealt with theologically and how — even in the midst of all the legitimate concentration on social-

ethical problems — the question of the church, its unity, its proclamation, its confession, and its worship, was drawn in and was seen
clearly in its significance for joint action in the social sphere.[37]

The World Conference for Faith and Order which took place
in Edinburgh in that same year did not make this kind of correction in its understanding of Christian and church cooperation.
It stayed with what had been said already ten years earlier in
Lausanne: practical cooperation between the churches is simply
a preliminary stage on the way to the ecumenical movement's
real goal; cooperation is possible even where there is no or only a
rudimentary theological and ecclesiological consensus; cooperation
is ecumenically relevant only when it is conscious of itself as a
means for reaching full fellowship of the churches in confession,
worship, and the office of the ministry, all of which are realized in
pulpit and altar fellowship and even more still in corporate union.[38]

Even later this view did not change substantially. Although the
third World Conference for Faith and Order in Lund (1952)
devoted far more attention than ever before to joint action and
emphasized strongly the necessity and the possibilities for church
cooperation,[39] here too, cooperation "in Christian action and mission" was still looked upon as a means of letting Christians "grow
into greater unity and more complete mutual recognition." [40]

But this estimation of cooperation was not limited to the sphere
of the Faith and Order movement. Also in the individual churches
and church families, practical cooperation with other Christians —
precisely where it *was* urged and practiced — was clearly accorded
only very peripheral significance for the understanding of and
efforts for unity; this was consistent with the general predominance
of the theological-ecclesiological motive. Typical of this is the
fact that even the Roman Catholic Church, in a time when it was
still trying to prohibit or drastically limit meetings with non-
Catholics in which questions of faith were dealt with, nevertheless
thought it could leave open the area of practical cooperation in
social matters and other general problems.[41] In principle, things
are hardly different in the *Decree on Ecumenism* from Vatican II
and the Ecumenical Directory, or in the just published "Guidelines
for Ecumenical Encounter" of the Lutheran World Federation's
Commission on Theology. Precisely where these documents recom-

mend and intend to render possible cooperation in the ecclesiastical
or secular spheres, they express an estimation of the ecumenical
relevance of practical cooperation that has not advanced beyond
that of Edinburgh.[42] It appears that the experiences of the Life and
Work movement and especially the insights of the World Conference of Oxford concerning the inseparability of practical cooperation and theological consensus have been able to make no real
inroads here.

The persistence of that view is one of the strongest indicators
of the degree in which the theological-ecclesiological motive won
the upper hand in the churches' understanding of and efforts for
unity, and how much it had crowded the commission motive out
of the focal point of ecumenical interest. True, it is emphasized
that efforts for church unity are not an end in themselves but
rather that what is ultimately at stake is to make joint action —
testimony and service — in the world possible.[43] But this cannot
gain credibility so long as joint action in missionary work and
social questions is represented simultaneously and in direct contradiction to it as a temporary *means* on the way to church fellowship.
The significance of this joint action does not reach into the ultimately decisive areas of theological and ecclesiological disagreement
or consensus, and it can be recommended for precisely that reason.

The new orientation of ecumenical thought and action to the
church's mission makes unavoidable a revision, or at least a clarification, of the view held up to now. This revision cannot be simply
a matter of expressing clearly and putting into practice the fact
that joint action in witness and service is the real goal of ecumenical
endeavor and church unity. True, that is fundamental and decisive
and is directly implied in the new orientation; but it is not enough.

Above all, the connection and relationship between theological
consensus and church unity on the one hand and cooperation in
witness and ministry on the other hand must be better understood
and acted on accordingly. Here the history of the ecumenical movement can teach us to avoid certain basic errors.

The first error is the idea that meaningful joint action is possible
if theological consensus and church fellowship are disregarded.
Joint action, whether in missionary work, evangelization, or the
social sphere, is possible and meaningful only when there is also a

common understanding of what is to be proclaimed as gospel and
how one is to act in the social sphere according to the gospel.
Efforts for joint action therefore lead ultimately to a concern for
the truth of the action, the question of "orthopraxis."

The second error is the idea that a church united on the basis
of agreement in confession, worship, and office of the ministry
will sort of automatically come to joint action in witness and
service. That will be the case only if the theological and ecclesiological consensus, which safeguards the church fellowship, in itself
is and remains aimed at making joint action possible in every new
situation and in this way maintaining church fellowship as fellowship in the service of reconciliation in the world. It is hardly necessary to search very far for examples of how the theological and
ecclesiological consensus, as it holds churches together today, no
longer possesses or more and more threatens to lose this action-
orienting quality, even where — as for example in Lutheranism —
it clearly had originally possessed this quality.[44] The consequences
are everywhere visible: divergent action in witness and service
results from the loss of action-orienting power on the part of the
traditional consensus and the consequent inability to "put it into
practice"; this leads to doubts about the existing church fellowship.
The increasing tendency to speak of "heresies" and reckon with
"schisms" resulting not from questions of doctrine or church order
but rather from the question whether Christians and churches have
in practice denied their responsibility for the world, points in this
direction.[45] Therefore, the search for forms of consensus aimed at
making joint action, witness, and service in the world possible is,
for all its difficulty, one of the most urgent tasks today both within
the individual churches and between them.

The difficulty of this task is very clear in the fact that — to isolate
a third error, already discussed above, the ideal of "uniformity"
and "likeness" — the question of cooperation and consensus must
be viewed under the aspect of the necessary diversity of Christian
witness and service. Therefore critical reflection on the limits of
the consensus necessarily belongs to the search for consensus as
that which gives to action the quality of joint action. Certainly
such reflection was never lacking. But for a long time and perhaps
even still it has been dominated too much by the question of the

"*possible* consensus" and consequently of the non-negotiable "minimum" and the attainable "maximum" — even where such concepts were rejected or studiously avoided. A way of thinking oriented to the commission and aimed at joint action will seek more the usefulness and so the "optimum" of the consensus. For it is entirely possible that the non-negotiable "minimum" will turn out to be meaningless and useless for joint action and — conversely — that the attainable "maximum" will hinder the diversity of witness and service. The key question of the "optimal consensus" would also affect the form and structure of the consensus. True, it must be possible to formulate the consensus. But that does not at all mean that it must take the form of a unified formula or consensus-text. A formulated consensus would be conceivable as a description of various views which are not harmonized in joint statements but rather whose convergence is made visible to a degree which safeguards the joint character of action even in the diversity of witness and service and which also makes it possible to recover it in cases of conflict.

Eschatological Orientation

Finally, the stronger orientation toward the church's missionary and social task will also bring along a strengthening and deepening of the relationship to the future, the eschatological orientation of ecumenical thought and action. It will reveal anew the bipolarity of the Christian endeavor for unity, the fact that ecumenical efforts must take the form not only of a one-sided manifestation of the church's given essential oneness, but also of action rooted in the hope for the promised unity.

This becomes clear when we temporarily split the "commission motive" up again into its components, the mission-evangelization motive, and the social-ethical motive, and ask how the church's missionary and social ethical task is understood today. In spite of all the differences of opinion in the present discussion and all the nuances pro and con, it can be said that in both areas, recent social ethics and recent theology of mission, the reference to eschatological expectation is one of the central and determinative moments.

On a broader basis, the Geneva World Conference for Church

and Society (1966) demonstrated that clearly for the area of social ethics. The joint formulation of that conference said that today the social mission of Christians and churches can no longer be limited to working for social renewal and justice "in and through the established institutions according to their rules"; it is much more a matter of working for the "transformation of society," for "basic changes" of the social structures.[46] The question of the theological basis of this new view led to eschatology: Christian action for reshaping society grows out of the expectation, based in Christ's cross and resurrection, of the world-transforming reign of God, which is already at work now. The report of the study group which dealt with "Theological Issues in Social Ethics" took up what had in part already been said in preliminary studies:

> The Christian lives in the world by the hope of the final victory of Christ over the powers of this age. He therefore sees the struggle for justice and true humanity in our time under the sign of this hope. In the fulfillment of time all nature, all the forces of human society, and human life itself will be transformed in a way beyond imagination.[47]

This eschatological perspective also marks the mission theology of the last two or three decades — perhaps even more emphatically and consistently.[48] The endeavor to overcome the crisis in mission work by giving it a theological and biblical foundation led, in the years during and after the Second World War, to renewed reflection on the close relationship between mission work and eschatology. Mission work is always "mission in view of the eschaton," as W. Freytag said even in 1942.[49] Mission work takes place in the span between Christ's already completed work and its hope for future consummation. It is not only an act of obedience, but also an "act of hope." [50] This eschatological aspect gave mission work new breadth and new dynamic and enabled it to overcome theologically certain traditional constrictions in the understanding and practice of mission work: the "pietistic" understanding, with its spiritualistic and individualistic narrowing of mission work, the "ecclesiastical" understanding, which practiced mission work as *plantatio ecclesiae,* the "philanthropic-evolutionistic" understanding, with its one-sided social-ethical view of mission work, and finally also the "apocalyptic" view, according to which the coming of the purely transcendent kingdom of God was to be expedited by mission work.[51] According to H. J. Margull's description,[52] the Willingen conference of the International Missionary Council (1952) marked the "penetration" of this eschatological rationale of mission work, the plenary assembly of the WCC in Evanston (1954), its "breakthrough." Margull interprets the first sentence of Section II from Evanston ("Jesus Christ is the Gospel we proclaim. He is also himself the Evangelist.") in exactly the sense:

> Evangelism is a christological datum, therefore it is an eschato-logical act. All missions, everything genuinely missionary, and every trace of missions are bound to Christ eschatologically and are therefore based on the messianic gathering of his people out of all nations with a view to his future and his manifestation at the end of history. The category of the missionary is the eschatological![53]

This brief sketch shows that when the commission motive becomes the central motive for ecumenical endeavor, the struggle for the church's unity necessarily appears, much more than before, in an eschatological perspective.

It must, however, be made very clear from the start that this inclusion of the eschatological aspect is in tension with what had been previously designated as the "ecumenical basic principle." This widely accepted principle, which gave the theological-ecclesiological motive for unity its clearest expression and also demonstrated its predominance over the other motives, defined the ecumenical task as the manifestation of the church's already given essential oneness. Thus it attempted to base the ecumenical imperative entirely on the indicative and to understand the imperative from the indicative. How is this related to the orientation of our efforts for unity to the eschatological promised and hoped for unity?

There can be no question that this basic principle expresses theological insights which cannot be compromised. It points out that the church and its unity are rooted in God's saving act and must constantly remain linked to it. It protects our efforts for unity from pure pragmatism and from the temptation to activism and works-righteousness. It awakens the consciousness of a profound

spiritual fellowship even between divided churches, lets us recognize the church of Christ even beyond the walls of our own
established churches, and thus prepares the way for ecumenical
encounter. Nonetheless, some critical inquiries must be directed
at that principle. This criticism takes three directions, which can
be portrayed with the aid of three labels.

First it must be asked whether this basic principle did not and
indeed did not *have* to give considerable reinforcement to the
historicizing *retrospective tendency* in the ecumenical endeavor.
Even where there was no basic agreement with the conception of
the "ancient undivided church," the idea of the "lost" unity proved
to be determinative all too often. Therefore, the historical questions
where, when, and why church divisions had come about played a
dominant role in most ecumenical studies and discussions; and
correspondingly the ecumenical imperative was widely put into
practice as a regressive dissolution of divisions or a retrospective
working out of how traditional antitheses are intrinsically complementary. True, the orientation of efforts for unity to the church's
given oneness was not meant in a historical sense, but nonetheless
it proved to be open to that kind of misunderstanding and so
could not counteract this retrospective tendency strongly enough.

The second question is whether the basic principle, when con-
verted into ecumenical praxis, did not necessarily lead to a tendency
which could be called an *objectification of the indicative*. The
church's given essential oneness appeared to be realized, even if
only partially, wherever there existed or came into being church
bodies united in faith and order. With that basic principle as a
beginning point, the temporary nature of these partial realizations
of unity and the need to challenge them with a more comprehensive idea of unity could not be emphasized clearly enough. As a
result of this weakness that basic principle could have the effect,
contrary to its real intent, of maintaining the ecumenical *status quo*.

The third critical inquiry is whether that one-sided orientation
of efforts for unity to the church's given essential oneness is not
to blame for the repeated threats of our ecumenical endeavor to
restrict itself to the attainment of a merely ecclesiastical fellowship.
The ecumenical imperative, as formulated by this principle, did
not point out beyond the church's unity to the church's commission

in the world, but rather was sort of "inverted" back onto the church itself, its inner essence and its outward appearance. This *inversion of the imperative* appears at least to be rooted in the call to make the church's essential oneness visible.

Of course it can be objected — rightly — that all these criticisms apply not to the basic principle itself but rather to definite misunderstandings of it and to tendencies which arise from those misunderstandings. But even when viewed in this way, these criticisms remain justified. So they do not negate the principle itself, but rather indicate the need to expand upon it and liberate it of its very noticeable biases. That is exactly what must be done!

The new orientation of ecumenical thought and action to the church's commission and the simultaneous intrusion of insights from social ethics and mission theology should lead us to view ecumenical endeavor, more so than in the past, in its eschatological orientation. It is in this sense that the above-mentioned Lutheran study document emphasizes that our efforts for church unity must take place "as it were between two poles, the oneness already given in God's saving act and the promised unity which has not yet been attained." [54]

Now this call is nothing new. In retrospect on the World Conference for Faith and Order in Lund (1952) and the assembly of the WCC in Evanston (1954), it was even said that already there "the breakthrough of the eschatological aspect for the consideration and treatment of the ecumenical problem" — "a fundamental novum in the ecumenical movement" — had taken place.[55] At Lund, in the larger context of a christologically oriented understanding of unity, the church was spoken of as the "pilgrim people," traveling on its way to meet the returning Christ, who will complete his work of salvation and judgment. The church, by virtue of the Holy Spirit imparted to it, now already belongs "essentially to the new age and the new creation" and therefore must "look beyond its historical forms to the full unveiling of its new being in the coming Lord." [56] At Evanston this "eschatological perspective" was once again emphasized.[57] If H. J. Margull's description is correct, the overall theme of the plenary assembly, "Christ the Hope of the World," was chosen, significantly enough, at the instigation of the eschatologically-oriented mission theology, and it provided the framework and the initiative for that emphasis of the eschatological aspect.[58]

Even though this eschatological aspect was judged by many as a "necessary background and perspective for the ecumenical quest," and even though it was emphasized that it must "absolutely not be lost sight of again," [59] nonetheless, in the time after Evanston it clearly receded into the background again. True, it is not entirely absent from the assemblies at New Delhi and Uppsala, but it very clearly no longer has the significance for understanding unity that Lund and Evanston had tried to give it. This too must be seen as an index of how dominant the "ecumenical basic principle" and along with it the theological-ecclesiological motive for unity were. So now it is necessary to take up again these starts from Lund and Evanston and to develop them further. The fact that now Roman Catholic theology also sees and affirms the eschatological nature of the church more clearly than in the past could help in this.[60] These starting points from Lund and Evanston have to be picked up and strengthened especially at two points:

1) When the eschatological aspect was drawn into the ecumenical problem at Lund and Evanston, the real accent lay on the fact that in the light of the eschatological expectation the temporary nature of our splits and divisions is revealed. "We must not assume that the divisions which now separate Christians from one another... coincide with the separation finally to be made by the Son of man. In this eschatological perspective all our human divisions are provisional." [61]

The importance of this aspect for our efforts for unity is obvious. But it must also be seen that, in the light of the eschatological expectation, not only our divisions but also our realizations of unity share in this fundamentally temporary nature. It is an old experience but one that perhaps has not been pondered enough that steps toward the realization of church unity can not only create new unity, but can also destroy existing unity. The history of the union movements, which in fact is simultaneously a history of new divisions, makes that clear. Therefore, the path of ecumenism cannot be seen as a steady dismantling of differences, a continuing process of growth in unity. On the contrary, it leads through new splits and divisions. That this is so and will always be so can be rightly understood and affirmed only under the eschatological aspect. It gives us the necessary freedom also over against existing realizations of unity; it makes an "objectification of the indicative" impossible and thus lets us make ecumenical steps and decisions even where they call existing fellowship into question.

2) The hope in which the church lives as the pilgrim people of God does not mean only that the church looks to the future, but it also evokes action. It is something that is not just "pro-spective," but also "progressive." It is in this sense that the dogmatic constitution of Vatican II says of the church: "the church strains toward the consummation of the kingdom and, with all her strength, hopes and desires to be united in glory with her King." [62]

It appears that this moment did not come completely to the fore in Lund and Evanston, even though it had been expressed clearly in the preliminary studies — for instance under the concept of "hasten forward." [63] This is the point at which we must now pick up the thread and continue.

The eschatological goal of the pilgrim people of God is already present in the Holy Spirit as the "earnest of our inheritance" (Eph. 1:14; 2 Cor. 1:22; 5:5). He is bestowed in advance and so he gives the ability and provides the power for the *anticipation* of the eschatological goal. Thus, the concept of eschatological "anticipation" has a necessary place in an understanding of the church as the pilgrim people of God.[64] Paul's statement on the Christian life's characteristic duality, as an unceasing, restless hastening forward that always takes place between past and future, aptly describes this legitimized anticipation in which the church also lives: "Not that I have already obtained this or am already perfect; but I press on to make it my own, because Christ Jesus has made me his own" (Phil. 3:12).

In fact, the church's whole life carries within itself this impulse of legitimized anticipation of the eschatological goal. Baptism is baptism into the death of Christ and simultaneously an anticipatory taking hold of the new creation. The Lord's Supper is the presence of the crucified Christ's sacrificial death and body and simultaneously an anticipation of the eschatological Messianic banquet. The righteousness of Christ which the Christian apprehends in faith is the "righteousness which we hope for in faith through the

Spirit" (Gal. 5:5). Our confession of faith and our theological comprehension take place in the anticipatory grasping of a truth which will be comprehended in all clarity in the eschaton.

Our ecclesiastical divisions and fellowship also carry this impulse of anticipation within themselves. Even if they are based on given confessions, traditions, or forms of church polity, they also are and remain anticipations of the eschatological separating and gathering.

The understanding of the church as the pilgrim people of God and — in this whole context — the insight into the anticipatory nature of our ecclesiastical divisions and realizations of unity would have to lead us to provide a legitimate place for the idea of anticipation in our ecumenical efforts. This certainly does not mean taking the whole ecumenical problem out of this world through an enthusiastic *tour de force*. This kind of a view of anticipation or a criticism of anticipation as though it meant this, would be foolish.

Of course, the danger of irresponsible anticipation does exist. It is present where there is a desire to pass over existing differences in a way that gives up entirely the quest for truth and error, gathering and separating. But this kind of anticipation would no longer be eschatological anticipation, since it overlooks the judgment nature of the eschaton. Irresponsible anticipation is also present where the anticipation is considered as the ultimate. Since this overlooks the eschatological difference and thus forgets the continuing provisional nature of everything anticipatory, it, too, would no longer be eschatological anticipation.

Quite apart from this danger, however, there opens up a broad area within which the principle of "anticipation of the promised" — understood as a supplement and a corrective to the principle of "manifestation of the given" — can and must be applied responsibly. It is that presently expanding area which is characterized by the fact that *on the one hand* basic points of agreement between divided churches have been reached or have become visible through doctrinal discussion, de facto fellowship, historical developments, and other factors, but *on the other hand* binding ecumenical steps and decisions are not made because the ideal of a comprehensive consensus does not become reality, historical divergences cannot be completely cleared up, and the existing ecclesiastical systems of order and organization demonstrate their durability. Of course it is as impossible to derive detailed practical instructions from this principle as it was from that "ecumenical basic principle" of the past! But this much can be said in the form of general guidelines: the fundamental affirmation of the eschatological orientation would give a legitimate place and theological significance to, as well as set up boundaries for the token transgressions and prophetic break-throughs of existing divisions which are inevitable in the present ecumenical situation and are therefore happening all around us. It would open up possibilities for church fellowship even where the examination of the present unifying elements does not fully warrant it and where historical divergences cannot be cleared up. It would help overcome the ever-recurring tendency to let doctrinal discussions and union negotiations run around, despite essential agreements, on the endless questions of explication, interpretation or application. Finally, it would endow our quest for consensus with that perspective of the future which is necessary if the consensus is to give direction and orientation to the even renewed commission of the church in the world.

— Translated by Jonathon Grothe

NOTES

1. W. A. Visser 't Hooft, "Ökumenischer Aufbruch," *Hauptschriften*, vol. II, Stuttgart-Berlin, 1967, pp. 210 f.
2. *Herder Korrespondenz*, No. 10, 1966, p. 481.
3. *Mission et Unité. Les exigences de la communion*, vol. I, Paris, 1960, p. 80. Today Yves Congar sees it this way, too. He says that in his description of the ecumenical movement in *"Chrétiens désunis"* (Principes d'un Oecuménism catholique, Paris, 1937, esp. pp. 171 f) he missed "the missionary dynamic of the ecumenical movement" (*Chrétiens en dialogue*, Paris, 1964, p. xxxv).
4. *Op. cit.*, p. 211.
5. R. Slenczka, e.g., speaks of the "ecclesiological point of departure" — be it of an institutional or an ontological nature — for viewing and dealing with the question of ecumenism within the Eastern Church (Ostkirche und Ökumene. *Die Einheit der Kirche als dogmatisches Problem in der neuren ostkirchlichen Theologie*, Göttingen, 1962, pp. 294 ff.)
6. Section I, 1 and 2; E. Schlink sees in this very point one of the most important things in common between the Roman Catholic ecumenism of

Vatican II and the more recent ecumenical movement. (*Dialogue on the Way. Protestant Report from Rome on the Vatican Council*, Minneapolis, 1965, p. 225).

7. Theses on "The Unity of the Church in Christ," *The Proceedings of the Third Assembly of the Lutheran World Federation*, Minneapolis, 1958, p. 86.

8. Visser 't Hooft, *op. cit.*, p. 211.

9. *Ibid.*, pp. 211, 214.

10. K. Barth, *Die Kirche und die Kirchen*, Munich, 1935, p. 7.

11. Visser 't Hooft, *op. cit.*, p. 41.

12. New Delhi, Section I, para. 58. (Unless otherwise indicated, subsequent pronouncements on the unity question from the ecumenical conferences and the assemblies of the WCC are quoted according to *A Documentary History of the Faith and Order Movement 1927-1963*, edited by L. Vischer, St. Louis, 1963.)

13. The overabundance of proof makes the quotation of any particular passages superfluous. Nevertheless cf. esp. the St. Andrew-Formula as presented and accepted in New Delhi: the "fully committed fellowship" which is to manifest the given unity of the church must reach out in its life "in witness and service to all" and make it possible "that all (sc. Christians) can act and speak together as occasion requires for the tasks to which God calls his people" (New Delhi, para. 2; cf. para. 11, 16). Cf. also the well-known formulation of the task of the Commission on Faith and Order, which names both in one breath: "to proclaim the essential oneness of the Church of Christ" and "to manifest that unity and its urgency for world mission and evangelism."

14. Visser 't Hooft, *op. cit.*, p. 140.

15. *Ibid.*, p. 145. This tendency to combine the church's unity and mission is expressed clearly already in 1935 in Karl Barth (*op. cit.*, pp. 6, 8); it can also be seen in the most recent collection of essays proceeding from the work of the Commission on Faith and Order. J. R. Nelson writes: "There can be no doubt that the visible unity of the church in all times and places is one of the strongest pieces of such evidence" (sc. of the truth of Christ's universality). This witness nature of church unity is also central for L. Newbegin: the church must "be recognizable to men as the one family into which it is God's will to draw all men by the Holy Spirit to be one body whose Head is Christ." (*What Unity Implies. Six Essays After Uppsala*, edited by Reinhard Groscurth, Geneva, 1969, pp. 111, 126).

16. E. Käsemann, "Das Interpretationsproblem des Epheserbriefes," in *Exegetische Versuche und Besinnungen*, vol. 2, Göttingen, 1964, p. 257.

17. E. Schweizer, "Die Kirche als Leib Christi in den paulinischen Antilegomena," *Theologische Literaturzeitung*, 1961, col. 254.

18. E. Käsemann, *op. cit.*, p. 263.

19. E. Käsemann, *Jesu letzter Wille nach Johannes 17*, 2nd ed., Tübingen, 1967, p. 104.

20. *Ibid.*, p. 117. "The earthly Jesus who associated with sinners and tax collectors and told the parable of the Good Samaritan has receded in the

distance along with the Pauline proclamation of the justification of the ungodly."

21. *The Lambeth Conference 1968. Resolutions and Reports,* London, 1968.

22. Published in Lutheran World, 1970, pp. 43 ff.

23. p. 120.

24. *Ibid.*

25. p. 49.

26. *Ibid.,* p. 44.

27. *Lambeth Conference,* p. 125; Lutheran Study Document, p. 43; *Uppsala,* para. 21.

28. *Uppsala,* para. 12. The Lutheran Study Document says: "From this focal point, the congregation gathered around the gospel and sacrament, there comes into being, in the midst of temptations and defeats and in the struggle against the pride-filled heart of each person, a larger unity embracing all races, classes and nations" (p. 43).

29. Edinburgh (1937), *Final Report,* para. 125; Lund, para. 113; New Delhi, Section I, para. 11.

30. Cf. e.g. the "likeness" in faith and confession, worship, doctrine, and administration of the sacraments, and ecclesiastical offices required by the World Conference in Edinburgh (1937) as the basis for unity *(Final Report,* para. 127-140).

31. *The Fourth World Conference on Faith and Order, Montreal 1963,* Report edited by P. C. Rodger and L. Vischer, New York, 1964, Section II, para. 64 (p. 57).

32. Para. 12, 13.

33. Evanston, Section I, para. 13; Lund, para. 71.

34. It was so stated in the basic principles of this movement, formulated already in 1913 (R. Rouse/St. Ch. Neill, *A History of the Ecumenical Movement,* London, 1964, p. 411).

35. *Faith and Order. Proceedings of the World Conference in Lausanne,* London 1927, pp. 398 f., 437 f.

36. *The Stockholm Conference. Official Report,* edited by G. K. A. Bell, London, 1926, pp. 18, 711.

37. In a pre-conference study on *The Function of the Church in Society* (London, 1937), J. H. Oldham, one of the leading men of the movement, had described Christian action as an "action springing out of the reality of the Christian fellowship, rooted in the obedience to the word the church proclaims, inspired and guided by its ministries, supported by its prayers, and examined and tested in intercourse with other Christians" (p. 192). After the conference he could say in retrospect: "Nothing stood out more clearly in the thought and work of the Oxford Conference than the recognition that the Church in its essential nature is a universal society, united in its one Lord and that in Him there can be neither Jew nor Greek, Barbarian nor Scythian, bond nor free" *(The Churches Survey Their Task: The Report of the Conference at Oxford,* London, 1937, p. 31).

38. Edinburgh, cf. para. 113-144; 171, 172.

39. Cf. para. 65-85; in addition para. 3, which formulated the so-called "Lund-principle," that the churches should "act together in all matters except those in which deep differences of conviction compel them to act separately."

40. Para. 61, cf. para. 36, 37. It could be asked whether the Commission for Faith and Order's own most recent study document ("Unity of the Church — Unity of Mankind") is not still closely tied to this view, even though the document has come into being against the background of the new orientation of the understanding of unity and is supposed to form the point of departure for the Commission's further study. In its outline and especially in the contents of its concluding section it at least gives the impression that ecumenical efforts aimed at the unity of mankind are, in the final analysis, once again being turned back instrumentally toward the unity of the church as the real goal.

41. Thus in the "Monitum" and in the "Instructions Concerning the 'Ecumenical Movement'" from the years 1948 and 1949.

42. Cf. *Ecumenism*, II, 12; "Ecumenical Directory" I, 6 e; "Guidelines for Ecumenical Encounter," in *Lutheran World*, 1970, pp. 55-56.

43. Cf. above, pp. 7 f., No. 13.

44. According to the Confessio Augustana VII, "consensus" ("consentire") means common action, and the unity of the church lies in this common action: "It is sufficient for the true unity (Lat.: *unitas)* of the Christian church that the gospel be preached in conformity (Lat.: consentire) with a pure understanding of it and the sacraments be administered in accordance with the divine Word."

45. In addition to W. A. Visser 't Hooft's address to the assembly in Uppsala ("The Mandate of the Ecumenical Movement," in *The Uppsala Report 1968*, Geneva, p. 320), cf. W. Bieder, "Die missionarische Bedeutung der *oikumene* und ihre drohende Verkirklichung," in *Evangelische Theologie*, 1962, pp. 187, 191 f., and J. C. Hoekendijk, "Die Welt als Horizont," in *Evangelische Theologie*, 1965, pp. 483 f.

46. "Message of the Conference," in *World Conference on Church and Society*, Geneva, 1967, p. 48.

47. In lieu of the many individual monographs, a quotation from J. Moltmann's *The Theology of Hope* (New York, 1967), may be sufficient: A Christian doctrine of social action must be developed in the "eschatological horizon of expectation of the kingdom of God, of his righteousness and his peace with a new creation, of his freedom and his humanity for all men." It is this expectation "which sets about criticizing and transforming the present because it is open towards the universal future of the kingdom" (pp. 334, 335).

48. Cf. esp. the comprehensive study by H. J. Margull, *Hope in Action*, Philadelphia, 1962.

49. *Reden und Aufsätze*, Part II, Munich, 1961, pp. 186 ff.

50. *Ibid.*, p. 190.

51. Cf. H. J. Margull, *op. cit.*, pp. 41 ff.

52. *Ibid.*, pp. 25, 35.

53. *Ibid.*, p. 7. The reports of studies and essays resulting from the work of the WCC, collected in the volume *The Church for Others*, Geneva, 1967, are a continuation — and indeed also a radicalization — of this line: mission is "participation in God's mission," i.e., in "God's redemptive work ... working out his purpose for creation"; it is "a turning towards the world, now seen from the perspective of hope, in the light of God's purpose" (p. 85).

54. Cf. *op. cit.*, p. 48

55. E. Kinder, *Der evangelische Glaube und die Kirche*, Berlin, 1958, p. 221.

56. Para. 17-19.

57. Section I, para. 19; cf. para. 5-9 and also the *Report of the Advisory Commission on the Main Theme of the Second Assembly. Christ — the Hope of the World*, New York, 1954, pp. 20 ff.

58. *Op. cit.*, pp. 27 f.

59. E. Kinder, *op. cit.*, p. 222.

60. In chapter VII the *Constitution on the Church* of Vatican II describes this "eschatological nature of the pilgrim Church." The article by H. Stirnimann, "Hoffnung — Struktur der Kirche" (in *Freiheit in der Begegnung*, edited by J.-L Leuba and H. Stirnimann, Frankfurt/Stuttgart, 1967, pp. 247 ff.), is interesting. He attempts to show, with special reference to Evanston, how close to each other the Roman Catholic and Protestant understanding of the church are at this point.

61. Evanston, Section I, para. 19; cf. Lund, para. 19, and the *Report of the Advisory Commission for Evanston (op. cit.*, p. 20). These passages take up what E. Schlink had said in his two addresses in Lund ("God's Pilgrim People") and Evanston ("Christ the Hope of the World"): "In looking forward, in awaiting the coming judge of the world and the redeemer, we will perceive the provisional nature, the lack of finality of many things which separate us." (In E. Schlink, *The Coming Christ and the Coming Church*, Philadelphia, 1968, p. 254, cf. pp. 245, 267 f.)

62. *The Church*, I, 5; H. Stirnimann (*op. cit.*, p. 256) points out that in the Latin the crucial phrases are even more apt: *ad regnum consummatum adhelat*, i.e., every breath of the church's life is for the coming kingdom; *totis viribus sperat*, i.e., it provides this hope with all its strength.

63. This concept, which is found in the Report of the Advisory Commission for Evanston and — emphasized even more — in E. Schlink's Lund address (*Report of the Advisory Commission, op. cit.*, p. 20, E. Schlink, *op. cit.*, pp. 254 f.), is not taken up into the official documents. They speak only of the fact that the eschatological expectation obliges and enables us to "work tirelessly" to overcome divisions and to "wait patiently and expectantly for the day when God shall sum up all things in Christ" (Evanston, Section I, para. 4; cf. Lund, para. 19, 133).

64. In the chapter on the "Eschatological Nature of the Pilgrim Church" in the *Constitution on the Church* of Vatican II it says: "The final age of the world has already come upon us. The renovation of the world has been irrevocably decreed and in this age is already anticipated in some real way" (Latin: *reali quodam modo anticipatur*), VII, 48.

Chapter 3

The Plurality of New Testament Theologies and the Unity of the Gospel as an Ecumenical Problem

The multiplicity of theologies cuts across denominational boundaries today more than ever before. This appears to minimize the significance of the denominational churches — and the unity of the church. It has apparently rendered joint church pronouncements and actions impossible; they are to be replaced by the work of theological schools or Christian groups.

This course of action appears not only to be required by the present day theological situation, but also to be legitimized by the New Testament. Historical-critical biblical research demonstrated that the New Testament writings, which traditionally stand together as a canon, a unified norm, actually advocate very diverse theologies. This insight led to this oftquoted conclusion for the ecumenical situation:

> The New Testament canon as such does not establish the unity of the church. On the contrary, as it is, *i.e.* as it is accessible to the historian, it establishes the multiplicity of confessions. The variability of the kerygma in the New Testament is an expression of the fact that already in earliest Christianity an abundance of different confessions existed side by side, following upon one another, merging with each other and making distinctions between themselves.[1]

Does this thesis do justice to the nature of the theological multiplicity within the New Testament and to the essence of confessions? That question has far-reaching significance.

If this picture of the structure of the canon is correct, it would define the canon's unique role in church history and in the church's present situation differently than it usually is defined in the Reformation tradition. In the second century, the Catholic church set forth the canon as the uniform basis of its tradition, but in the course of church history, its authority was repeatedly pointed against the church. Extremely diverse ecclesiastical groups came into being by appealing to it. And today scientific biblical research on the one hand may well be the most important theological factor in bringing the Greek Orthodox and Roman Catholic churches as well as churches of Reformation origin together for theological discussions, but on the other hand it is simultaneously the source of new and profoundly contrary views within the Protestant churches. The New Testament has the power to unite and the power to separate, because it contains, for everybody, the basis of being a Christian. But the question is: Does it separate because it is interpreted divergently on the basis of different hermeneutic presuppositions or because it is in itself theologically self-contradictory?

Thus today the theological plurality of the New Testament presents a problem as pressing as it is exemplary in the ecumenical search for the unity of the church and its gospel.

THE PLURALITY WITHIN THE NEW TESTAMENT AND ITS ECCLESIOLOGICAL CONSEQUENCES

The theological plurality of the New Testament has been observed and has had an ecclesiological effect for a long time already. To begin, three typical examples from church history may illustrate this. Even before the canonization of the New Testament Scriptures was completed, Marcion appealed to Paul and Luke against the writings emanating from the earliest apostles, in which he found the same Judaism as in the church of his time, and finally he determined a canon and a church which was consistent with his Paulinism. Eventually though not just in opposition to him, the Catholic church canonized the *Corpus Paulinum* together with the Gospel according to Matthew and the Epistle of James. But from the very beginning it allowed the canon with its many layers and meanings to be authoritative only and always in conjunction with ecclesiastical tradition, summarized in the *regula fidei,* and the ecclesiastical teaching office, legitimized by apostolic succession. Luther began anew with Paul. In the Epistle to the Romans he finds the center of the gospel, from which he can understand the entire Scripture. From the viewpoint of this center some New Testament writings — the Epistle of James, the Epistle to the Hebrews, and the Apocalypse — appear to him as of secondary importance. He makes Scripture, understood in this way, the sole norm of ecclesiastical action and argues against the necessity of combining it with the church's tradition and teaching office. But this *sola scriptura* is meaningful only so long as it is joined to the double hermeneutical principle of the *analogia scripturae sacrae* and the *analogia fidei.* And the latter, the central meaning which is the basis for interpreting the rest, is described in the Book of Concord — with the reservation of course, that these confessional documents themselves submit, in a dialectic circle, to the judgment of Scripture.

These typical examples from church history offer three fundamentally different solutions to our problem: Marcion bases the unity of the church on one portion of the New Testament writings, extracted by historical and literary reduction. But the Catholic church establishes itself on an overarching harmonization of th⁻ canon's multiplicity by ecclesiastical tradition. Finally, the church of the Lutheran Reformation relates itself to the center of Scripture, which holds the New Testament's multiplicity together from within and makes distinctions according to content. When Catholic theologians like Hans Küng explain that they view "the entirety of the New Testament as pertinent testimony to the revelation-event in Jesus Christ" and thereby "let each individual witness" stand as "true, but differentiated in its orientation to this saving event in Christ," while Protestants are "eclectic," this applies to Marcion and to modern Protestantism, but not to Luther.[2]

The *historical-critical biblical research* which began in the 18th century handles the multiplicity of the New Testament in a fundamentally different way. It takes the multiplicity of the New Testament and first reconstructs the history of earliest Christianity; then, in a second step, it extracts from this over-all view of New Testament history the lines which lead to Christian existence in the present. Thus differences between the New Testament writings and between their underlying traditions are worked out more and more distinctly, because the various phenomena of the early history of Christianity are reflected in these differences and so in this way a picture of those phenomena can be extracted.

Ferdinand Christian Baur drafted the first "purely historical" overall picture around 1840. According to him the New Testament writings are witnesses to history of the development of ideas which ran its course from the sharp antithesis between Paul and the earliest apostles to the synthesis of Catholicism about the middle of the second century. The constant element in this development, which unites the New Testament writings inwardly and remains significant for the present, is the idea of Christianity, which emerges more and more clearly in the development of this dialectical process. At the high point of historicism around 1900, the "history of religions school" finds different religions reflected in the New Testament writings; Palestinian and Hellenistic Christianity each clothe the prophet and teacher from Nazareth with different myths. These mythologies are refined especially by Paul and John through theological reflection. The true religion, which underlies all these temporally conditioned developments, is the "plain gospel of Jesus," which corresponds to mankind's original religion. Since that time the ongoing historical analysis has brought to light still more differences within the New Testament.

Bultmann and his followers carried the historical analysis within the history of religions school on to its extreme possibilities. But theologically he sees that what is essentially at stake in the New Testament is not religion, but rather the kerygma, which constitutes faith and establishes the church. For him the center of the New Testament is the kerygma, which Paul and John properly describe theologically, while other New Testament writings, as also the "apostolic fathers," distort it.

On the basis of this new theological orientation, Bultmann's student Ernst Käsemann could bring this view of the New Testament into the ecumenical discussion and into confrontation with the traditional ideas of canon, church, and confession. Thus the hypothesis quoted at the beginning of this essay was formed; Käsemann argues it further as follows:

> If the canon is binding as it stands in its entirety, then the various confessions may claim for themselves longer or shorter passages, well known or unknown New Testament authors with more or less historical justification. Their right to claim them is fundamentally indisputable and in particular cases can be proven.

But in Käsemann's opinion, this historical statement minimizes the theological significance neither of the differences in the canon nor of confessions; for

> the canon is not simply identical with the gospel, and it is the Word of God only in so far . . . as it is and becomes gospel. To that extent, then, it also establishes the unity of the church . . . But what the gospel is the historian can no longer answer with a historical statement; only the believer, convinced by the Spirit and heeding Scripture, can determine that. Thus the unity of the church, too, is never out in the open but exists always and only for faith.[3]

Thus the unity of the canon as of the church is secured through a kerygmatic actuality which comprehends the one truth of the gospel.

The Catholic theologian Patrik V. Dias, in his book, which has been widely read in the ecumenical movement,[4] portrays the direction of research which leads to Käsemann's theses as the "Protestant position"; thus and in presenting such an extreme alternative, he at any rate makes the problem especially clear.

To make it possible to judge the differences in the understanding of gospel and church which exist *within the New Testament* or which the New Testament assumes and addresses as existing in New Testament Christianity, the following would be necessary. The differences would have to be *clarified exegetically* in detail, coming to grips with the discussion concerning them in the historical critical school of biblical research; for when the differences appear as contradictions, it is often due to biased exegesis. This exegetical inquiry is not possible in the framework of this article; we can only refer to other studies. In order, then, to be able to judge the real theological differences within the New Testament properly, we must gain *a perspective appropriate to the subject matter.* To find this perspective and its corresponding categories, we first pose the question: how did Paul, in his time, see and solve this problem which is confronting us; the problem of theological multiplicity and the unity of the church and its gospel?

PAUL'S VIEW OF DIVERSITY WITHIN THE ONE CHURCH

When we direct our question to *the Pauline Epistles,* it is surprising to see what a variety of forms of ecclesiastical practice and doctrine Paul allows within the church. For him, the *variety* is a *diversity* which is given through the freedom of faith and the many forms which the Spirit's work can take; but behind it stand one Lord, one Spirit, one faith, and one church (1 Cor. 12:4-6; cf. Eph. 4:1-7).

Several examples may serve to illustrate the extent of this diversity which is encompassed within the unity. In Romans 14-15 the congregation at Rome is called upon not to see a divisive gap in the *different behavior* of the "strong" and the "weak," in the one's freedom to live as he likes and the other's asceticism, but rather to bear it in love as the expression of the one faith. No one has the right to judge the other; each man "stands or falls before his own master" (Rom. 14:4). There is only one limit: "whatever does not proceed from faith is sin!" (Rom. 14:23). Therefore — and this should be noted for the purpose of illustration — the congregation as congregation cannot actualize its unity through joint actions in matters of political and economic judgment.

On the contrary, the congregation must accept its members going differing socio-political ways; for it lives "by faith" and no longer according to the law (Rom. 10:4). Paul advocated such an extensive freedom of choice for the individual Christian in the ethical shaping of his life that the pneumatics in Corinth could outdo him, as it were, by recasting the old formula for life according to the law, "What is lawful?" into the slogan, "All things are lawful for me" (1 Cor. 6:12). But Paul had not meant the emancipation of the individual, but rather the (eschatological) freedom which results from faith's being bound to its new Lord: "All are yours, and you are Christ's, and Christ is God's" (1 Cor. 3:23). Therefore for Paul the ecumenical *koinonia* encompasses the congregations in Palestine, which live according to the Mosaic law, just as much as it does the Hellenistic congregations, which live independent of it — so long as the law is not made the principle of being a Christian.

In its worship services, too, the congregation should, in great freedom, allow each of its members to render it services according to his respective gift (1 Cor. 12 and 14). The form of the celebration thus becomes very flexible; the only decisive thing is that it be shaped by the Spirit which confesses Jesus as the Lord and acts in accord with the meal instituted by him (1 Cor. 12:3; 11:17-34). Accordingly, Paul bases his congregations' system of order on the charismata, but without any polemicizing against the presbyter-system which was coming into use at the same time in other areas of the church; for him there is room for both in the *koinonia* of the one *ekklesia*.

Now *theology* — and this cannot be said too clearly — fits into this picture too. In Corinth, for example, other missionaries, Apollos and teachers who appealed to Peter, were active in the congregation after Paul had founded it. When members of the congregation note that they have different kinds of theology, some of them follow the one and some the other (1 Cor. 1:12). But Paul makes it clear to the congregation that Apollos is a partner in the same ministry as he himself is, because he effects faith too: "What then is Apollos? What is Paul? Servants through whom you believed" (1 Cor. 3:5). Furthermore, Paul knows that in many things Peter, and especially James, the brother of the Lord, hold a different theological opinion than he does. These differences break out, *e.g.*, in the Antioch incident (Gal. 2:11-14). But Paul emphasizes all the more that Peter and James start from the same earliest traditional kerygma that he does and that at the apostolic council they recognized his formulation of the kerygma as essentially the same as their own (1 Cor. 15:11; Gal. 2:6-10).

Paul does not conceive this multiformity of life and theology in the Hellenistic sense, as a free unfolding of individuality and of traditions on the basis of an underlying syncretism. This becomes clear in the following: Paul does not admit that which was so much a matter of course for the Hellenistic environment that Josephus takes great pains to show that it exists in Judaism, too, for Paul denies that the diversity in the individual congregations or in the church as a whole displays itself in the formation of groups, as in Hellenism and Judaism. He vehemently forbids the formation of schisms, groups around individual teachers or *haireseis,* theological schools (1 Cor. 11:17-21), while Josephus emphasizes that there *are haireseis* in Judaism too, namely groups such as the Pharisees, etc.[5] Paul rejects these social phenomena familiar to his environment because they grow out of the group's or individual's desire for self-realization and not out of the ministry to all. The diversity is legitimized if it is effective as a plurality of ministries, through which the one Lord pursues all, each in his uniqueness, and wins them for the faith (1 Cor. 12:4 ff.).

PAUL'S VIEW OF THE LIMITS OF DIVERSITY IN TERMS OF HERESY

If Paul understands the broad diversity of forms of doctrine and life in this sense, then what at first glance is surprising becomes understandable, namely that *he also repeatedly pronounces a clear "No" to a "different doctrine"* and to its manifestations in the congregation's life. The motive and goal of a considerable portion of his epistles are such injunctions: next to the apodictic "No" to the nomistic Judaism in Galatia stands the renunciation of the Judaistic pneuma-movement in Corinth and the Judaizing Gnosticism in Collossae.

These findings pose the question more pointedly: what obliges Paul on the one hand to assert the koinonia despite all diversity and on the other hand to draw a clear dividing line despite all points of contact? An answer to both arises when we pursue the negative side of the question: *What constitutes the essence of the ecclesiastical-theological phenomena which Paul in his day rejects?*

Paul has no uniform *designation* for them. He characterizes them mostly, in conformity with the Old Testament-Jewish style, by using compounds of pseudo- or hetero-. It is first the Pastoral epistles which speak of a *hairetikos anthropos* and thereby bring the term closer to the later meaning "heretical." At the same time, they form a concept for correct doctrine and speak of "the healthy" or of "the good" doctrine. The forms of orthos, "right," familiar to philosophy, appear nowhere in the New Testament (except Gal. 2:14 and 2 Tim. 2:15); they are all conceived of from the point of view of the right system.

Paul characterizes these phenomena, which for the sake of brevity we now will call "heresies," not with a term, but solely by their subject matter; he names *two essential characteristics:*

First: the unity in the diversity results from the kerygmatic unfolding and application of the one gospel, but heresy brings *"a different gospel,* another Christ, a different spirit," 2 Cor. 11:4; likewise Gal. 1:6-9; "a different gospel, which in reality is not a gospel."

This false gospel is — this is the second characteristic — *the expression of a refusal to believe.* False doctrine is not an intellectual aberration, but rather an existential closing of one's self over against the gospel. The false teachers in Galatia shun the cross, which signifies the break with the old ego and with the world (Gal. 5:11; 6:12). The opponents in 2 Corinthians boast of their religious potency, pass themselves off as *homines religiosi,* and do not live by faith (2 Cor. 10:17). They also use the fact that the congregation provides for them as their confirmation; they base their existence on something human — all-too human (2 Cor. 11:7-11). These charges, which in the latter New Testament writings often become very massive, intend neither to defame morally the man who holds a different theological opinion nor to dispute the heretic's human decency. According to what was said above, heresy is not a different theological opinion, but rather a false gospel, which by necessity corresponds to a denial of true faith.

Now it is important to see that these two charges apply neither to the self-understanding of the false doctrine nor to the impression which it makes upon the congregation. The teachers in Galatia and Corinth against whom Paul writes want to bring a better gospel than he brought. They do not wish to break up the church, but rather to make it attractive in society. The pneumatics in Corinth desire finally to make the true pneumatic knowledge and freedom accessible to the congregation. The Judaizers in Galatia seek to make the Pauline semi-Christians into the true people of salvation

(Gal. 3:29). The false apostles in Corinth want to belong to Christ in a higher degree than Paul (2 Cor. 10:7). Again and again, the advocates of the false gospel claim for themselves not only the pneuma, but also the authentic apostolic tradition (Gal. 1:17; perhaps 2 Cor. 11:5; 1 Cor. 12:3). Thus heresy presents itself as the higher truth and is readily received as such (1 John 4:3 characterizes heresy as a form of anti-Christianity!)

Thus the question arises: *how does Paul recognize these phenomena and prove that they are heresy?* That is, at the same time, the key ecumenical question: how do doctrine and life become church-dividing? This is, in general, the question as to the center which bears the diversity and repels that which is truly alien. Paul answers this question in the following steps:

1. As his criterion, he first names *the gospel entrusted to him as an apostle.* He received this gospel *in a twofold form.* In 1 Cor. 15:1-8 he characterizes his gospel as a traditional formula: "I preach to you the gospel . . . ; for I delivered (as tradition) to you what I also received (as tradition). . ." Then the paradosis of the Easter kerygma is quoted. On the other hand in Gal. 1:12 he characterizes his gospel as the revelation imparted to him before Damascus: "I did not receive it (as tradition) from man . . . , but rather (I received it) through a revelation of Jesus Christ." Here the gospel is not received as a formula, but rather as the understanding recognition of the crucified one (Gal. 1:15-16).

Thus the gospel occurs on the one hand as a traditional formula and on the other hand as a present revelation. Both belong together! Because the end-time revelation happened and happens though hidden in history, the gospel comes as a traditional formula; but because it is nevertheless the eschatological revelation through which man becomes completely new, it comes also as a pneumatic event.

2. In keeping with this its essence, Paul applies the gospel as a criterion with regard to content in this way. He does not judge whether a sermon or doctrine which has arisen in the congregation agrees with the apostolic gospel on the basis of coinciding formulae, but rather *by whether the soteriological center of the gospel is properly assimilated.* For example, the Judaizers in Galatia may

very well recite the formula of 1 Cor. 15:3-5; all they want to do is complete faith in Christ by adding the obligation to the law. Therefore Paul dismisses them with the sentence: "If there is righteousness through observance of the law, then Christ has died in vain" (Gal. 2:21). Or Gal. 5:2: "If you receive circumcision, Christ is no longer of any significance for you." Accordingly, in 2 Corinthians he says against the false apostles: Whoever commends himself in this manner is not a servant of Christ (2 Cor. 10:12-17; 11:10-11). These missionaries, too, no doubt say much that is the same or similar to what Paul says, but with them every word has a different orientation. Consequently, the criterion by which Paul judges content is the crucified and resurrected Christ as the conclusive and exclusive mediator of salvation, as the gospel testifies.

This criterion is not meant quantitatively; it is not the minimum, outside of which anything goes. On the contrary, it is the center which should determine everything and by which, therefore, everything is to be judged. Paul can judge in this manner because he does not measure according to a theological aggregate of statements or of doctrines in which each individual point has differing value, but rather he judges according to the basic principle: what does not proceed from faith is sin. Heresy confronts him by no means as a fullblown system, but rather as an isolated intention and assertion, and Paul endeavors to expose its roots himself.

Thence follows 3): *Only through a specific theological interpretation of the gospel with a view to the situation* is it possible to recognize and to demonstrate that a phenomenon is heresy according to the above-named criterion of content. Heresy grows out of the current situation of the church. For example, the pneuma movement in Corinth resulted from the crucial encounter of the gospel with Hellenism. Heresy accompanies the gospel in its advance into the world; it is the most effective and therefore the most dangerous means of immunizing the world from the gospel. Thus it is no accident that for Paul heresy proves to be an impulse which drives the theological interpretation of the gospel forward. The controversy with the Judaizers, for example, was without a doubt a very vital motivating force in the interpretation of the gospel as justification, even if the doctrine of justification is most certainly not merely an anti-Judaistic polemic.

Thus in the controversy with heresy, seen from the outside, one interpretation of the gospel opposes the other. How is one to know which interpretation is proper? Paul does not decide in an authoritarian manner, by appealing to his apostleship; instead he makes his case by argumentation. In what sense is his argumentation convincing? It discloses *the knowledge of faith;* it can only be accepted in such a way that the one who accepts it himself becomes different through it. In this way Paul avoids the tension between the alien authority and the autonomy of the hearer which is discussed so much today. In this sense Paul's powerful argumentation won, by all indications, the congregations in Galatia and Corinth for his interpretation, *i.e.* once again for faith.

Accordingly, what the truth of the gospel is in a concrete situation vis à vis heresy cannot be worked out from traditional tenets, but rather can only be witnessed to and confessed as the knowledge of faith. It is in this sense that "the discerning of the spirits" is a charisma (1 Cor. 12:10). When something is confessed jointly in this sense, the koinonia of the church is actualized, as it happened, *e.g.,* at the apostolic council between Paul and the earliest apostles.

THE NATURE OF HERESY

When we compare our findings up to this point with three other interpretations of the Pauline criterion, what we have seen as the sustaining and decisive center in Paul becomes clearer still.

In the *history of religions school* it was held that for Paul a theoretical doctrinalism which abstracts from life, or a Jewish legalism, or Hellenistic speculation, is heretical. What is true and authentic is the intensity of the religions-cultic experience.

Just as those men developed the criterion out of the antithesis: dogma and religiosity, so *Helmut Köster,* in his *RGG* article on heresy[6] and in an article in the Bultmann Festschrift,[7] derives it from the antithesis between mythical tradition and historicity of existence. In his own words:

> Thus heresy originates in this, that the radical nature of the historicity of the new existence is not recognized, that the revealer's death on the cross is not taken seriously as the shattering (demythologizing) of that security which desires to

> withdraw from historical existence through religiosity, piety, and theology.... Tradition as such becomes heresy as soon as one tries to repristinate it. (pp. 71, 76).

It is the task of Christian theology and proclamation constantly to interpret anew the traditional language, which as such is mythical.

Turning to the positive side, *Gerhard Ebeling* offers a third version when he explains: "The basic tradition — we can simply say: Jesus Christ — is to be differentiated from the traditions in which the testimony to Jesus Christ eventually appears." [8] Therefore the unity of the church is real always and only in so far as this origin of the church in the believing relationship to Jesus Christ is a present reality (p. 77). Thus the unity can always and only be confessed in the present moment, and cannot be expressed in the content of joint formulations. "The actual consentire suffices for the true unity of the church, even if it does not lead to the explication of the consentire." [9]

Following along the lines of this view of the Pauline statements on church and heresy, with which he expressly agrees, *Klaus Händler,* in an article typical of the present state of the discussion,[10] attempts to bring the problem of the denominational confessions to the forefront by explaining: The fact that the Christian faith is historically conditioned makes it necessary that it be expressed in a confession, and nevertheless this confession is again and again abrogated by the very historical nature of Christian comprehension of the truth; for the truth must be expressed anew for the present, moment by moment. Now the fact that it is historically conditioned in every present moment is certainly an essential side of faith and truth and thereby of the problem of denominations and confessions. But if it is viewed as the only side, it leads to an abstraction which does justice neither to the reality of confessions nor to the Christian message. That can be seen in the concept of heresy here presupposed.

If these three suggestions are compared with our findings, one thing becomes clear: these descriptions of the criterion or center correspond to a great extent to the characterization of the gospel in Gal. 1; here it actually is religious experience, induction into the historicity of existence, confrontation with Jesus Christ as the tradition itself. But each of these sketches conflicts with the description of the gospel in 1 Cor. 15; here Jesus can no longer be separated from the course of his life, death, and resurrection and thus from the traditional testimony. This is not merely the issuing of a proclamation through which the historicity of existence is attained; on the contrary, this testifies to a revelation in history for a faith which must be lived in history. If we want to describe the center in Paul which bears the unity of the church in the diversity and divides from heresy, then the statements of Gal. 1 and 1 Cor. 15 must be combined and the gospel must be defined simultaneously as a historical tradition and a pneumatic-kerygmatic force.

Then, of course — this is the other side — it cannot be captured in a static *regula fidei* which describes truth once and for all. *The early Christian development* which leads from Paul to the incipient Catholic church of the second century leaned in this direction.

DIVERSITY AND ITS LIMITS IN POST-PAULINE NEW TESTAMENT WRITINGS

After this orientation in Paul it is natural to ask: *do the other New Testament writings* share his view of the diversity, the unity, and the boundary line of the proclamation's possible expressions? Here we can only give a few allusions and references in answer to this question.

The rest of the New Testament writings, without exception, came into being in the post-Pauline period, *i.e.*, between 65 and 100. Unlike Paul, none of these authors comes to grips directly with the course of developments in the entire church. The increasing diffusion, the premature violent end of the ecumenical figures, Paul, Peter, and James, and the fall of Jerusalem all led to separate ecclesiastical developments in each particular area of the Roman Empire. During this time each of *the evangelists* recorded the Jesus-tradition, which until then had been handed down as oral tradition, in written form for his own congregation, in order to give it a lasting bond with the root of its existence, namely Jesus' appearing. Luke brings about this bond more through historical continuity by drawing in Acts a line from Jerusalem, where Jesus' earthly work ended, to Rome: Only what has issued forth from this line

deserves the name church. John, on the contrary, ties the congregation to Jesus' appearing by the kerygmatic interpretation of that
appearing: the Johannine discourses of Jesus express what Jesus'
speaking and acting have to say to the post-Easter congregation.
Mark and Matthew each bridge this gap in yet a different way:
Mark with the help of the Messianic secret, Matthew in the method
of his mission command (Matt. 28:19-20). Beginning from these
points of departure, each of the evangelists offers the history of
Jesus in his own theological interpretation. These theological conceptions of the four evangelists are very diverse, as the redaction-
historical examination of the gospels in the last twenty years has
ascertained. The discussion has not yet ended on the question
whether Luke and John stand in conflict with each other or, as
appears to me, complement one another like two poles. The same
problem, to refer briefly now to the rest of the writings, has been
pondered for a long time concerning the theological relationship
between the *Gospel according to John,* with which the Johannine
Epistles belong, *and the Apocalypse of John.* The Apocalypse and
First Peter address a situation of Christians in society which has
changed considerably over against what it was in Paul's time.
Both characterize Rome with the biblical picture-word "Bablyon"
(1 Pet. 5:13; Apoc. 14:8 *et al.*). But the call in First Pet. 2 to subject
one's self to the emperor simultaneously continues the tradition of
Rom. 13, while the Apocalypse can only warn against the Anti-
Christ in Rome. While *First John* uses formally dualistic antitheses
to summon to an uncompromising eschatological existence vis à vis
the world and speaks of no ecclesiastical office, the *Pastoral Epistles*
introduce the idea of a "virtuous Christian life" in the world and a
consolidation of the system of ecclesiastical offices. *Hebrews,* like
Romans, establishes and clarifies the Christian faith by beginning
from the viewpoint of the law but does not start, as Paul does,
from the law summarized in the decalogue but rather from the
cultic regulations.

Thus as these few allusions show, at every step along the way
differences can be demonstrated between the New Testament
writings of the post-Pauline period, and the question arises again
and again: are these variations caused by the author's individuality,
his special traditions and the situation to which his proclamation

is addressed, or are they theological contradictions? This question could be answered in detail only through exegetical studies. One important indication of the fact that these writings essentially belong together is the fact that they relate their proclamation to the church in fundamentally the same way Paul did. None of them intends to give forth a theological norm for the whole church which everyone must recognize. Rather, each solicits the obedience which is from faith, which only God can give. Therefore, they, too, exclude only the proclamation and theology which bring "a different Christ" and thus destroy faith (1 John 4:1-3; 1 Tim. 6:20; 2 Tim. 2:18). At the same time it is an established fact for all of them that, according to the will of its one Lord, the church in the whole world is a unity and that this unity must be expressed in a corresponding attitude in the lives of the church's members in the individual congregation and in the relationship between the congregations. The New Testament's last word chronologically on this question is also its most pressing: John 17:20-23!

THE PLURALITY OF THEOLOGIES AND THE UNITY OF THE GOSPEL IN THE NEW TESTAMENT

With the help of the perspective which we have gained in Paul and which the other New Testament writings fundamentally share, we can now attempt to describe how the question of the *plurality of theologies and the unity of the church and its gospel in the New Testament* can be answered for our historical-theological view in its entirety.

1. In Paul's view *the multiplicity of theologies does not fundamentally place the unity of the church in doubt;* for no congregation prescribes for itself a standard theology and no New Testament writing intends to offer such a theology. There were neither Pauline nor Johannine congregations! First Corinthians' remarks on the situation in the congregation show that very different theologies were expressed in the proclamation in Corinth just a few years after the foundation of the congregation. Already for this reason we can see that the New Testament's different types of doctrine and proclamation do not reflect denominational churches! At the most one

could ask whether kinds of the doctrinal differences in the New Testament writings correspond to or are even the basis of doctrinal differences between denominational churches. It appears to me that neither the one nor the other proves true. The difference between the Lutheran and the Roman Catholic church, for example, is neither prefigured in nor — not even indirectly — based on that between Paul and Luke, even if a line does lead from Luke to the incipient Catholic church. Denominational differences are motivated by differences within the canon only in very small measure. To give an example, one could probably say that the fourfold division of the ministry in the Reformed tradition follows Acts' system of congregational order, but that the congregationalist view of the ministry follows the picture of the charismata in 1 Cor. 12.

The relationship of the theologies which speak out of the New Testament writings to the faith and life of their congregations can be defined positively in this way: Without exception, we find the theologies of the New Testament writings in the form of a proclamatory address. Without a doubt they take up traditions of their respective congregations and address their own special situations. But they do not simply mirror what is believed and practiced in the congregation; on the contrary, they want to shape both. From the very beginning, the proclamation of the New Testament writings intends to be a constitutive and normative testimony to the Christ-revelation and the formation of the church. They were preserved and finally canonized because they won recognition for this claim from their hearers and therefore were read again and again in the worship service, even though, indeed, *because* their content was always above that which was empirically present in the congregation's faith and life.[11] This relationship between proclamation and congregation was misrepresented in the history of religions school and the line of research which followed it by the overemphasis of the proclamation's dependence on congregational traditions.

What role do the current traditions in the congregation play? Paul appeals again and again to binding traditions which were passed on in the congregation, namely the Jesus-tradition, which later was incorporated in the gospels, the traditional formula of Jesus' life, death, and resurrection and of his majesty (*e.g.*, 1 Cor. 15:3-5; Rom. 1:3-4), and paraenetic traditions. These traditions do not grow spontaneously out of the congregation's life; on the contrary, they are formulated and handed down by responsible witnesses and teachers. They are neither formulae fallen down from heaven nor purely pneumatic, self-validating kerygma, but fixed testimonial formulae, and yet they are always oriented to a pneumatic-kerygmatic application and therefore can be modified. In keeping with their nature, they are not simply recited in the New Testament, but rather are always passed on in the framework of a proclamation to a specific congregational situation. Even the gospels do not simply recite logia of Jesus, but pass them on in a framework and a form which makes them understandable for the current congregational situation. Thus it is proper that the gospels were brought into the canon side by side and were originally designated as "the Gospel according to Matthew, and according to Mark."

From that it follows for evaluating the plurality: *the statements of the New Testament writings* are not to be viewed as fragments of a static system of doctrine but rather as dynamic forces with a definite direction in the *movement from the center outward to a goal.* The criterion against which they themselves want to be measured is whether they, each of them in the situation to which they address their proclamation, speak from the same center, Jesus, and have that same ultimate goal, faith. And here "Jesus" is never merely a cipher but rather always the one whom the gospel tradition testifies to in connection with the Easter tradition.

Consequently, the New Testament's theological plurality does not lead us to seek a minimum standard theology but rather the center of the proclamation and of faith, which gathers the church together and unifies it.

2. To be able to ascertain that center, *the causes of the differences in the theological statements of the New Testament writings* must be considered in detail.

a) As was already made plain, the New Testament writings are not timeless treatises but are without exception *directed to specific situations* as a proclamatory address, whose purpose is to establish and to refine faith. We are not supposed to conclude from this that the New Testament is merely the church's first book of sermons and that only the common root of these sermons, the historical Jesus, has lasting significance. On the contrary, the New Testament contains the enduring and constitutive testimony to Jesus' earthly work, to Easter and to the formation of the church, but it contains it in a kerygma related to specific situations. Therefore the statements of the individual writings and of the various strata of their traditions can be compared and related to our present day only in such a way that their whole complex relationship to their original situation is transformed into another relationship to another situation. When doing this, especially the salvation-historical difference between the situation of Jesus' earthly work and the work of the exalted one in the post-Easter church must be kept in mind. Furthermore, we must see the profound shift that occurred in the situation to which the proclamation was addressed when it passed from Israel to the Gentiles, out of the world of Palestinian Judaism into the world of Hellenistic syncretism, and from the first generation to the second generation of the Christian church.

b) Likewise the *nature of the statement* must be considered. The effect of baptism, for example, is variously expressed as a missionary promise for him who is called to baptism (Acts 2:38; John 3:5), as a report of a consummated act of baptism (Acts 19:5-6) and as proclamation of what happens in baptism for every one who is baptized (Rom. 6:1-13). Only when this orientation of the statement is considered can the statements be compared.

c) The fact that the New Testament writings or groups of writings employ *diverse terminologies* must also be considered. The event of salvation, *e.g.*, is designated in the Synoptics as the forgiveness of sins, in Paul as justification and reconciliation, in John as new birth. The same process is always meant. And yet the phrases are not absolutely identical; each of them respectively emphasizes especially one aspect of the process and places it in a particular context of ideas, in keeping with its origin in Jewish, Hellenistic, and Christian traditions. In Bultmann's *Theology of the New Testament* many statements are identified too hastily and, under the assumption that mythical patterns have been taken over in them, are reduced by existentialistic interpretation to a few basic anthropological formulae. But the New Testament witnesses have not simply taken over terminologies; on the contrary, like every ideologically powerful movement, they themselves have assimilated the available material and have shaped the language. When the New Testament writings developed such different terminologies in such a short time, this not only manifests the movement's ideological power, but also indicates that here an event is being testified to which is always greater than the formulae which describe it. A proper evaluation and comparison of the New Testament statements is therefore possible only when the respective terminology is decoded and translated, while its complex content is preserved.

d) Finally, it must be borne in mind that the individual New Testament witnesses not only are determined by special traditions and by the situation to which their proclamation is addressed, but they also formulate their statements with *a particular theological intention.* Whoever has an eye for the author's special theology will find in the variety of the New Testament statements primarily the diversity of theologies rather than the expression of different confessions.

It is possible to see and judge theological differences properly only when these historical factors which cause variations in the New Testament statements are considered.

The variety within the New Testament comes forward then essentially in the framework of *two larger questions:* (1) how is *Jesus' earthly work,* especially as recorded in the Synoptic gospels, related to the gathering together of the church through the *post-Easter message of the resurrected one* as, for example, Paul reflects it? If the above mentioned factors are applied in the comparison, then it can be seen that the New Testament's diverse theological sketches, first and foremost those of Paul and John, take precisely this picture of Jesus as their point of departure and understand it, to a great extent consciously, as the criterion of the spirit-effected proclamation. (2) The other larger question is: how are the kerygmatic theologies of *the post-Pauline New Testament writings* related on the one hand to Paul and on the other hand to the earliest post-canonical literature? In the Bultmann school, for example, the thesis is repeatedly advocated that Lucan theology conflicts with Paul's and is "incipient Catholic." But Johannine theology, seen from the viewpoint of Luke and incipient Catholicism, is "heretical."

These theses are based on biased exegesis, which interprets the New Testament writings virtually against each other. From the results of my own study,[12] it appears likely that the borderline between "apostolic" and "incipient Catholic" or Gnostic voices in early Christian literature surprisingly enough lies pretty much where the ancient church eventually, often with far too little justification, drew the boundary of the canon.

(3) If the kerygma of the New Testament writings is compared with that of the Catholic theology of the second century and with that of Gnosticism, *the common center of the proclamation* can be delineated, from which all the New Testament writings speak. At the same time then, an individual statement's relationship to this center becomes a criterion against the background of which marginal statements within the New Testament itself stand out clearly. The Catholic exegete Franz Mussner [13] gives a good critical survey of the present exegetical-polemical discussion of this question of the center of the New Testament. He says: "as this kind of 'center' one could perhaps point to the gospel of the in-breaking of the eschatological time of salvation in Jesus Christ." [14] In the concluding portion of his *Theologie des Neuen Testaments nach seinen Hauptzeugen,*[15] Werner Georg Kümmel finds "the center of the New Testament" and sees it in the twofold message

> that God has made his salvation, promised for the end of the world, begin in Jesus Christ and that in this Christ-event God has confronted us and wants to confront us as our Father, who desires to rescue us from captivity in the world and make us free to act in love.[16]

These definitions agree to a great extent with the one which has come to me as the result of exegetical analysis. According to it, the center which we are seeking can be described as follows:

a) If the *relationship to the Old Testament* is examined, then it can be seen, as has often been observed, that already in the apostolic fathers that relationship takes on a character fundamentally different from what it is in the New Testament writings. In the New Testament, certainly more or less pronouncedly but definitely uniformly, the view is advocated that with Jesus the eschaton was present in the form of the fulfillment of the Old Testament promises and the abrogation of the Old Testament law. On the other hand, for incipient Catholicism from First Clement to Justin, the fulfillment and the abrogation are given for the time being only in part. The prophecies are divided up between the first and the second coming (Justin, *Dial.* 14,8; 32, 2 *et al.*), while for Paul they are already fulfilled completely, even if in a veiled manner (2 Cor. 1:12), to be realized visibly in the Parousia. What Paul says of the end of the law is limited to the ceremonial law (Justin, *Dial.* 43, 1). Thus for the apostolic fathers Christian existence no longer has a really eschatological character. But in Gnosticism the eschatological abrogation of the Old Testament turns into the dualistic antithesis.

b) A common basic line of New Testament *Christology* corresponds to this definition of Jesus' coming and his church's appearing from the Old Testament. The common element — after what has been said above about terminology this is no longer surprising — is not to be found in the designations of majesty. Of course, Jesus is designated, e.g., as Son of God throughout all the strata of the New Testament, but its meaning varies widely. But what is shared is the testimony about Jesus' "way," to which the gospels point and from which the epistles start: Jesus, sent from the God of the Old Testament, was active among Israel as the promised one, died for the sin of all men, was raised from the dead to a personal life in communion with God, and thereby was exalted to be the ruler in God's place at the end of time, who carries out his reign now in a veiled manner through faith and will do so visibly at the end. It is not a contradiction but rather a development, when in the Hellenistic church a pre-existence is added onto this "way" of Christ about which the Synoptic gospels are silent, even though it was known to the evangelists.

c) Now furthermore, the New Testament is in remarkable accord on the decisive point of giving a soteriological interpretation to this gospel, which in line with the four gospels describes the Easter kerygma. Christologically, it mediates to men full salvation through faith. Even Revelation and the Epistles of James, as Adolf Schlatter already showed,[17] advocate this mediation of salvation through faith. Of course, James cannot describe adequately what faith is, because he employs theology as analysis of the empirical situation and does not speak kerygmatically. For faith is, as Paul above all makes clear, the vessel which is shaped by its content. Man's salvation, which faith now mediates, is described in the New Testament writings with different concepts, but on this point they all say together that man becomes new because his relationship to God is healed: In this sense the Synoptic gospels and Acts describe the event of salvation as the forgiveness of sins, John and others as "new birth," but Paul as reconciliation and justification. (Mark 2:1-7; John 3:3, 5, 14-16; 1 Pet. 1:3; Rom. 3:28; Phil. 3, 4-10; James 2:12-13; Apoc. 20:15.) Among these descriptions, "justification" occupies the central place theologically; for the formula "righteousness of God" expresses more directly than any other formula what the word "God" says for the Old Testament: Through his promise God binds himself to man in a legal relationship and man lives from this relationship. God shows himself to be righteous when he acts according to this promise, and man is righteous when he lives in keeping with this relationship, which has been given to him, i.e., by faith.

d) And so, according to the entire New Testament, *salvation is mediated through the word,* which in its care is a promise addressed to man. Confrontation with Jesus in the days of his earthly life and the rites of Baptism and the Lord's Supper do not stand independently alongside the word, but rather contain the word as their decisive factor and are encompassed by the word. They, like the word, do not work through the attitude of the man receiving them, but rather are effective in and of themselves, because they do not make pronouncements *about* God but rather contain God's own powerful and effective promise (1 Thess. 2:13; 2 Cor. 5:21; James 1:18; 1 Pet. 1:23).

In conclusion, let us draw from our findings *the consequence for the present-day situation in the ecumenical movement!* What does this insight into the structure of the New Testament canon contribute to the path of the churches to each other? This much is clear: the diversity of the forms of doctrine and life which, according to the New Testament, are possible within the koinonia of the ekklesia, is broader than we, in our ecclesiastical traditions, generally think; for the sustaining and dividing center is also deeper and more stratified than traditional formulae let one surmise.

Therefore, ecumenical koinonia cannot be attained by relativizing confessional differences on the basis of a theological plurality which cuts through confessions nor by reducing common theological statements to the least common denominator. It also cannot be produced by setting forth the fact that faith is historically conditioned, in order to justify the expression of faith confessionally, or the fact that the comprehension of the truth has a historical character, which yet again and again transcends its confessional expression.[18] Both the theology which makes itself individually independent of the tradition and the conscious incorporation of confessions and of their witnesses into the historicity of existence arise out of the thought of the modern age — but also, admittedly with different surface symptoms, out of the activity of Jesus, which calls each individual to faith in his own situation and abrogates the generalizing law. Therefore these ecclesiastical-theological phenomena and insights of the modern age can yield fruit for the ecumenical discussion if they are seen in the proper perspective.

We attempted to gain this perspective from the New Testament, above all from Paul. If the confessional churches seek the truth and the help of the gospel for our time, and examine as well the divisions existing today, with this perspective of the ministry to mankind charged to them today, they will be led out beyond that which once, for the sake of the truth and the ministry, separated them. Then the koinonia, which everyone today recognizes as an obligation, can be realized openly. Koinonia means uniformity today less than ever. Koinonia means first that the denominations unconditionally recognize each other as church and understand their different ways of serving as a multiformity of the one ministry; today more than ever this multiformity of the ministry is appropriate for a multiform world. P. V. Dias, in the above-mentioned book,[19] recently set forth this multiformity of the ministry and therefore of the church's life on the basis of the New Testament as the task and the promise for ecclesiastical action in the present. But this koinonia presupposes that the depth and breadth of the gospel, from which the multiformity of the New Testament proclamation radiates, be comprehended together and with a view to the pressing tasks of the present. The Epistle to the Ephesians suggests this path to the formation of the ecumenical church: "... that you may have power to comprehend with all the saints what is the breadth and length and height and depth, and be able to know the love of Christ which surpasses all knowledge" (Eph. 3:18-19).

— Translated by Jonathon Grothe

NOTES

1. E. Käsemann, *Exegetische Versuche und Besinnungen* I. Göttingen, 1960, p. 221.

2. H. King, "Der Frühkatholizismus im Neuen Testament als kontroverstheologisches Problem," *Theologische Quartalschrift* CXLII (1962), 402-423, quotation from p. 423.

3. E. Käsemann, *op. cit.*, p. 223.

4. P. V. Dias, *Vielfalt der Kirche in der Vielfalt der Jünger, Zeugen und Diener.* Freiburg/Basel/Wien, 1968, pp. 63-73.

5. *Hairesis* here, just as in Josephus, does not yet have the meaning "heresy" or even "denomination," so that a negative legitimization of the denominational split from 1 Cor. 11:19 is exegetically wrong.

6. H. Köster, "Häretiker im Urchristentum," RGG³ III, 17-21.

7. H. Köster, "Häretiker im Urchristentum als theologisches Problem," in *Zeit und Geschichte,* Bultmann Festschrift, Tübingen, 1964, pp. 61-76.

8. G. Ebeling, *Die Geschichtlichkeit der Kirche und ihre Verkündigung als theologisches Problem,* Tübingen, 1954, pp. 67-68.

9. G. Ebeling, *Wort und Glaube,* Tübingen, 1960, pp. 161 ff.

10. K. Händler, "Haben wir nicht alle einen Gott?" *Evangelische Theologie* XXIX Jg. (1969) No. 10, *Uberlegungen zum Konfessionsproblem,* pp. 534-555.

11. H. von Campenhausen, *Die Entstehung der christlichen Bibel,* Tübingen, 1968, works this out more clearly than it has been seen up till now and summarizes it aptly on pp. 380 ff.

12. The problem is discussed in §18 of my *Geschichte der Apostolischen und Nachapostolischen Zeit,* Göttingen, 1966²

13. F. Mussner, " 'Evangelium' und 'Mitte des Evangeliums'. Ein Beitrag zur Kontroverstheologie," in *Gott in Welt,* Festschrift für Karl Rahner, Freiburg/Basel/Wien, 1964, vol. I, 509-511.

14. *Ibid.,* p. 511.

15. W. G. Kümmel, *Theologie des Neuen Testaments nach seinen Hauptzeugen,* Göttingen, 1969.

16. *Ibid.,* pp. 294 ff.

17. A. Schlatter, *Der Glaube im Neuen Testament,* Stuttgart, 1905, 1965.⁵

18. *Op. cit.,* p. 14.

19. See footnote 4.

Chapter 4

Roman Catholic
and Lutheran Relationships

To speak seriously of the recovery of unity between the Roman
Catholic and the Lutheran churches will seem to most members of
both churches unrealistic and perhaps even visionary. The doctrinal
differences are many and well known, differences of practice and
devotional attitude both wide and deep, and the emotional tensions
strong and easily stirred. That the accumulated differences of four
and a half centuries should be bridgeable in our time seems an
opinion born in wishful thinking, nourished by romanticism, and
utterly without awareness of the facts.

Yet what has happened in the world and in both churches is so
significant and far-reaching that we can without exaggeration
speak of a new theological and ecclesiastical situation. The development of biblical and historical studies, the rise and progress
of the ecumenical movement, and the altered situation of the
church in the world, create new situations and give new perspectives which require that traditional outlooks and relationships be
radically reexamined.

Catholic and Lutheran churches are being prodded to reexamine
and rethink their traditional relationships because of cultural
changes which have taken place in the modern world. For men of
the Middle Ages, faith in God was a part of the atmosphere in

which they lived. The one who challenged theistic ways of thinking had to make a radical break with his cultural surroundings. The church as steward of God's revelation had a place at the very center of human existence and possibilities of immense influence in almost every area of human life. The situation today is different.

There are still many countries where the church as a social grouping or as an institution is listened to and perhaps even respected. But nowhere does it command men's minds and loyalties as it once did. In many countries it is regarded as an institution of the past, preserving venerable and even valuable traditions, but with no constructive message for a world dominated by science. For many educated and humane persons the church is a reactionary institution and a negligible social group, standing for values which are to be rejected, supporting policies and programs which inhibit human growth and freedom, and siding with the powerful and privileged against the poor and disinherited.

Today, moreover, belief in God is neither as widespread nor as potent as it once was. Many still confess faith in God, even in orthodox Christian terms, but for many, if not most, believers faith is something which concerns only man's inwardness, and has nothing decisive to say in the important decisions of life. Many believers are theoretical theists and practical atheists: God's Lordship is conceded in the realm of private religion, but it has small influence in the things that really matter, world affairs, national politics, social life, work, and recreation.

Many churchmen continue to think and work as though the church were still a dominant force in culture, respected and secure. They struggle to maintain their privileges or to reinstate those that have been lost, as though the developments in the world since the French revolution were only a bad dream. Such churchmen can ignore the contributions of biblical and historical scholarship as the passing fads of academicians, dismiss ecumenical theological discussions as dilettantism, suggest that the leaders of the ecumenical movement are sentimentalists if not false prophets, and continue to occupy the entrenched positions of the past as though nothing significant had happened since 1600.

There are, however, also churchmen who are aware of what has taken place in the modern world, who sense the loss of Christian substance in the churches, and who yearn for a church that seeks the fullness of the gospel and obeys the missionary command of Jesus Christ. For them the life of the church in exile in the modern world is both painful reality and missionary opportunity. Christians in Hitler's Germany, for example, both Catholics and Evangelicals, in prison or under persecution, found a unity in Christ in spite of confessional differences. They realized the weakness and spiritual poverty of the churches and discovered their strength not in the impressive tomes of the theologians, nor in institutional or liturgical triumphalism, but in the presence of the living Jesus Christ in the midst of his people. The recognition that God is not limited or bound by the blunders and sins of his people gave rise to a new hope for the unity of the church, the unity in love and in the service of Christ that is necessary if the church is to accomplish its mission in the world.

Another factor working for the disappearance of traditional differences, questionable as it may be to theologians, is the indifference of many people today to the heritage of the past. At its worst, this attitude sees the values and achievements of men of the past as sharing the inadequacy of their plumbing arrangements or their modes of transportation, and therefore to be superseded as rapidly as possible. But even among those who do not regard skill in gadgetry as a mark of cultural superiority, there is a tendency to see the scientific revolution of the twentieth century as so radical as to invalidate the thought forms and values of earlier times. A development that relieves the church of the weight of the dead past can be welcomed, but there is, of course, danger that contempt for the past may blind us to the insights of great theologians and impoverish us through our inability to learn from the past.

The situation of the church today is so much different from what it was at the time of the Reformation that we do well to heed what it suggests about the need for renewal in the churches. We can no longer assume that the churches have matters well in hand, and that the Christian mission is being carried out in obedience to Christ. The church indeed bears a startling resemblance to the disobedient Israel of the Old Testament and needs repentance and renewed dedication to its mission. We cannot afford the illusion of success, of institutional self-righteousness and of theological complacency, but must recognize our poverty and seek renewal for effective mission.

A second aspect of the changed situation is the impressive new perspectives given by biblical and historical studies. The examination of the scriptures in their historical setting has always been a part of the church's theological enterprise, but it has been carried out with greater thoroughness and sophistication since the Renaissance of the 16th century, and particularly in the 19th and 20th centuries. This kind of study has had a disturbing effect upon traditionalist theologians and has therefore generated opposition in the church, but the accumulated effect of this kind of work has been of great value to the church and its theological enterprise. More than any other single factor it has prepared the way for a common understanding of the message of the Scriptures and for widespread appreciation of the richness and complexity of the theological tradition of the early church.

It has shown first of all that the New Testament does not have one homogeneous theology, but that it comprises a complex of theologies, each witnessing to what God has done in Jesus Christ from its own distinctive perspective, out of its own historical situation, and with its own vocabulary and method.[1] Instead of trying to find out which of the church's theologies corresponds most adequately to the theology of the New Testament, we can accept theological pluralism as a sign of the wealth of the church's heritage. This does not of course mean that all theological positions are equally good — "all have won and all shall have prizes" — and that controversy or even discussion are now to give way to a relativistic good will and agnosticism. The concern for truth continues to be the prime occupation of theology, but in an awareness that truth is more various and richer than earlier generations have supposed.

Systematic theologians concerned with the questions of theological method and language have come to a somewhat comparable position.[2] It is now clear that all theological statements are relative to the historical situations out of which they have emerged and from which they derive their categories and their method. Certain theological issues, such as the doctrine of Christ or of the Trinity, have been thought through more strenuously than others in the history of theology. Certain theological statements, such as the Nicene and Chalcedonian creeds, have been given special dogmatic status by the church because of their usefulness in clarifying certain aspects of the Christian proclamation. But these statements can not be interpreted without reference to the situations which called them forth and to the intention of the theologians who formulated them. Thus the church is involved in constant historical and theological reflection upon its message as it wrestles anew with the problem of formulating that message with clarity and force for its own generation.

The awareness of the plurality of theologies enables the theologian to understand some theological controversies of the past in greater breadth and depth. He can recognize that some controversies became heated precisely because both sides were conscious of understanding the gospel and aware of biblical support for their position. We can now see that the resolution of such controversies is not properly done by the abolition of one of the positions, but rather by the discovery of a perspective which does justice to the truth in both of them. Such positions are often not antithetical but complementary.

The development of new perspectives on the message of the scriptures and on the meaning of theological statement has virtually resolved some of the traditional controversies between Catholics and Lutherans. The doctrine of justification by faith was the subject of furious controversy in the 16th century. Theologians of both traditions can agree today because of the contribution of biblical and historical studies. Catholics can recognize that the bishops at Trent believed that they were rejecting the Lutheran position on justification, but in fact condemned a misunderstanding of it.[3] Differences in the understanding of the term faith as well as misinformation and suspicion about the teaching of the reformers contributed to this inadequate theological encounter. Today biblically informed theologians in both traditions can agree on the teaching of the New Testament concerning justification by grace through faith, and can agree on theological formulations of the doctrine without denying or betraying their theological heritage. That this agreement is not known or acknowledged by every theologian and churchman in both traditions is not disproof of the statement but only testifies to the time lag between the work of specialists and more popular presentations.

The doctrine of the priesthood of all believers also occasioned brisk dispute in the 16th century. Catholic controversialists saw this doctrine as a denial of the ministerial priesthood and rejection of the sacramental system and hierarchical structure of the church. With respect to some Protestant groups, some of these suspicions were well grounded. Exegetes of all denominations recognize today that the priesthood of the faithful as participation in the priesthood of Christ is basic to the apostolic understanding of the life and function of the church. Thanks to biblical interpreters and to the work of theologians like Congar, this doctrine is no longer an object of suspicion in informed Catholic circles and is in fact expounded in the Constitution *Lumen Gentium* of Vatican II.[4]

Few theological controversies have engendered more bitter dispute than those about the Lord's Supper. Catholics and Lutherans have exchanged serious charges and argued vehemently about the question of sacrifice in relation to the Supper and about the problem of the Real Presence.

The teaching that the mass is a sacrifice, an unbloody repetition of Calvary, evoked from the reformers some of their strongest denunciatory language. Catholics responded with equal vigor and eloquence. For some centuries it appeared that the church would be permanently divided by this teaching. Studies in the scriptures and in the history of religions have, however, in this century, provided an understanding of sacrifice which promises resolution of the disagreements. In his book *The Fullness of Sacrifice*,[5] Bishop Hicks offers an interpretation of sacrifice and its fulfillment in the ministry of Christ which meets the doctrinal requirements of both Catholics and Lutherans. The initial break-through in this discussion took place in the meeting of Faith and Order at Edinburgh in 1937,[6] and produced a document still too little known among theologians, not to speak of wider circles. The new perspective satisfies the concerns of both groups, stressing the sacrificial significance of the death of Christ, the communication of its benefits in the Last Supper, the once-for-all character of Christ's death, and the Supper as the movement of God's love to men.[7]

The Doctrine of transubstantiation also seemed destined to be a permanent rock of offense. Lutherans understood it to be not only an assertion of the presence of Christ in the sacrament but also the specification of the mode of the presence, at best an unnecessary attempt to explain the inexplicable, at worst an essay in theological physics or chemistry. Catholics saw in rejection of the doctrine a denial of the presence of Christ and therefore the reduction of the sacrament to a memorial. Today Catholics are pleased to learn that Lutherans assert the real presence in the sacrament, and Lutherans are equally pleased to learn that the doctrine of transubstantiation is an emphatic assertion of Christ's presence and not an insistence that faith accept a specific metaphysical explanation of the mode of the presence.[8]

In addition to the areas where disagreements of long standing can be overcome, there are also important areas where the theology of both traditions is converging. This convergence is a product of several factors but chiefly the result of a common openness to sound critical scholarship in biblical and historical studies. Whereas even a generation ago there were separate Catholic and Protestant translations of the scriptures, today common versions are in use in many countries and their usage is growing. Catholic and Protestant exegetes disagree with one another, but the disagreements are very often not on confessional lines; the same schools of interpretation will often be found in both Catholic and Protestant circles.

Some of the most important areas of theological convergence can be briefly sketched.

The last half century has seen the growth of remarkable similarity in the understanding of the church. The opening chapter of the Constitution *Lumen Gentium* discusses the church as the mystery of God, a community which results from God's purposeful activity in human history, and not simply the result of political and sociological factors.[9] This kind of thinking and the vocabulary in which it is expressed have much in common with the theology of the Orthodox churches. It is also strikingly parallel to the emphasis on the church as an event in the history of salvation, an emphasis to be found in many theologians in Protestant traditions.[10]

The theology of chapter two of *Lumen Gentium* also offers notable parallels to Orthodox and Protestant reflection on the church.[11] The emphasis upon the church as the people of God corresponds to the theology which has developed out of ecumenical studies, especially in the Faith and Order movement. It stresses the communal rather than institutional aspects of the church's life, sets in sharp relief the mission of the church as an extension of the work of Christ, makes clear the church's involvement in the historical and social processes of its time, and helps to move away from the defensiveness and triumphalism which have marred so much of the self-consciousness of church bodies. The image of the people of God has Old Testament connotations which are especially poignant for the denominations in this stage of their existence, reminding both of God's judgment upon a disobedient people, but recalling also the grace and love which enable us to understand how we with all our faults and failures can still be the people of God.[12]

The understanding of Scripture and its relationship to Tradition is another important area of convergence. The polemics of the 16th century polarized most Catholic and Protestant theologians in this area, but the discussions of the ecumenical movement have begun to draw them closer together.[13]

Studies in the apostolic period, a growing acquaintance with the theology of the orthodox churches, together with the awareness that the apostolic tradition is prior to the formation of the biblical canon, have made Protestant theologians more conscious of the problems of interpretation which attend the exegesis of the New Testament. The growing importance of hermeneutics in modern theology has opened up areas of theological concern previously obscured by confessional polemics. Roman Catholic theologians have on their part accepted the methods and results of historical critical study and thus moved closer to Protestants in their understanding of Scripture. The Apostolic Constitution of Vatican II accepts an advanced critical posture and thus moves Catholic study of these problems into the same area occupied by the ecumenical discussion.[14]

The study and experience of the churches has been moving them toward convergence in other areas as well. The crisis of faith, prayer, and worship has caused realistic theologians of all traditions to reexamine the meaning and function of the church's worship.[15] Basic questions about the place of the ordained ministry and its relation to the priesthood of all believers have been raised in most church groups, and have lead to reexamination of many traditional positions.[16] Missiologists of all traditions have moved toward greater understanding of each other as well as toward a common understanding of the mission of the church in the world.[17] Catholics and Lutherans alike have learned from the free church traditions much that is valuable about the importance of individual freedom in the life of the church. The realization is growing in all groups that an individual must have religious freedom if he is to be able to have faith in the sense of the New Testament. Much religious immaturity and regimented behaviour has been mistaken for genuine faith in the churches, at great cost to the development of genuine community and individual personality. That the churches recognize the errors of the past in this area is one of the more hopeful signs of common understanding in the church today.[18]

The reader will note that nothing has been said about convergence in the understanding of papal primacy and infallibility or the place of Mary in the church. These two points remain difficult problems whose resolution we cannot now foresee, but even here encouraging developments can be noted. The action of Vatican II in treating the Marian question in the context of the doctrine of the church was an important decision from the ecumenical standpoint, indicating the determination of the Catholic church to discuss this question with other Christian churches, and having the effect of cooling off some of the more extreme developments in Marian devotion.[19] Marian theologians have since the council moved toward ecumenical discussion, another fruitful by-product of the council.

Chapter three of *Lumen Gentium* reaffirms the Vatican decree of 1870 concerning papal primacy and infallibility but also introduces the notion of collegiality of bishops.[20] This exploration of the role of bishops in the teaching and governing of the church offers hope of a development which may lead in time to an understanding of papacy more acceptable to Orthodox and Protestant Christians. The chapter on collegiality opens the way to increased participation by bishops in the governing of the church and to a corresponding decrease in the power of the Roman Curia. There are many indications that this process of decentralization is under way: the establishment of the Synod of Bishops and the vigorous participation of many bishops; the increasing number of bishops from out-side of Italy in the Curia itself; the growing number of matters which are given to diocesan bishops for decision; the increasing importance of regional and national episcopal conferences; the reaction of many bishops to the encyclical *Humanae Vitae*. It may well be that this encyclical, while certainly not intended to bring papal authority into question, has done more to stimulate inde-pendent thought and action among Catholics than any other docu-ment in this century. The reaction of bishops' conferences and groups of theologians has been a stimulus to the growth of collegial thinking and action.

There are, of course, forces at work opposing these changes. Many curial officials struggle against these shifts in power, and many bishops, including some who voted for change at the council, continue to administer their dioceses with minimal concessions to the new ways. Many lay Catholics, including prominent figures like Jacques Maritain [21] or Evelyn Waugh, have opposed the Council's program and appealed for keeping to the old paths. But it is also clear that many laymen and most younger priests and nuns have decided for the new ways and at a pace which must alarm those who prefer the *status quo*. Some see great dangers within the Catholic church if there is serious tension between over-cautious leadership and the vehement desire for change on the part of younger Catholics.

The opposition to ecumenism and renewal in the Catholic church is, of course, nothing new. Institutional inertia and the nursing of resentments against outsiders have become familiar through socio-logical studies of institutions and social groups. In the Catholic church they have been allies of entrenched curial control of doctrine and practice. The promulgation of papal primacy and infallibility did not result in one man rule, an administrative impossibility in an organization as large and complex as the Catholic church, but rather in a collective primacy and infallibility, almost always in the name of the pope, but not always with strict attention to the limitations of papal authority specified in the Vatican decree. Thus a theologian could be dismissed from a teaching post or refused the right to publish because the theologians advising the Doctrinal Congregation did not approve of his theology. The ritual and ceremonial of worship were subjected to strict controls, the regulations concerning marriage, fasting, or penance given out, interpreted, and judged by Roman authorities.

We should recognize that there are forces within the Lutheran church also which work against the recovery of unity. As in the Catholic church, these forces can rely upon substantial resources of accumulated hostility toward, and suspicion of, the other tradition, can depend upon institutional inertia and the conservatism of church members, and can oppose change in the name of loyalty to the principles of the reformation. The most potent of these forces in the Lutheran tradition is confessionalism, a force all the more dangerous because it is so difficult to distinguish from true confessional loyalty. This form of churchmanship overlooks the apologetic purpose of the Augsburg Confession and the reformers' intention of preserving the true Catholic tradition, and reads the Confession not as a Catholic but as a sectarian document. Lutheranism is then seen not as an attempt to preserve sound Catholicism through the rediscovery of the gospel but simply as opposition to the Catholicism of Rome.

Confessionalism of this kind leads to the polarization so common in Protestantism in which one secures condemnation of a doctrine or practice simply by showing that Catholics approve of it. Such Lutherans see the problem of Christian unity in comparatively simple terms: it will be achieved when all other Christians adopt the doctrine and practice of the Lutheran church.

Those who fear that the recovery of unity will mean the absorption of all churches into a super-church, and the loss of all the values of the denominational traditions, should be reminded that responsible ecumenism today renounces the recovery of unity through surrender and looks rather for convergence. It is to be fervently hoped that church unity will not mean the imposition of one pattern of life upon all, but a unity in Christ which respects legitimate variations in doctrine, practice, devotional patterns, and life styles.[22] Nothing of real value from any church tradition should be lost, but be preserved for the enrichment of the church's worship and service.

Optimism in the quest for unity is one of a Christian's duties. It is difficult to be optimistic in view of the human capacity for bungling and our history of self-righteousness, defensiveness, and suspicion of others. There are many factors on the scene today which inhibit optimism. But the Christian is called to obedience to a Lord who wills the unity of his people in love, in order that their mission to the world may be credible and effective. Therefore, despite disappointments and discouragements, the Christian looks forward with confidence to the realization of the hope that "at the name of Jesus every knee shall bow ... and every tongue confess that Jesus Christ is Lord to the glory of God the Father."

NOTES

1. The literature in this area is extensive. Standard works are Rudolf Bultmann, *Theology of the New Testament*, New York: Scribner and Sons, 1951; and E. F. Scott, *The Varieties of New Testament Religion*, New York: Scribner and Sons, 1947.

2. Here also there is an extensive literature. Many of the problems are discussed in John McQuarrie, *God-Talk*, New York: Harper and Row, 1967.

3. *Lutherans and Catholics in Dialogue: I. The Status of the Nicene Creed as Dogma of the Church*. Published Jointly by the USA Committee of the Lutheran World Federation and the Bishops' Commission for Ecumenical Affairs, 1965.

4. *Lumen Gentium*, 10-12.

5. F. C. N. Hicks, *The Fullness of Sacrifice*, London: Macmillan, 1930.

6. Leonard Hodgson, *The Second World Conference on Faith and Order*, New York: Macmillan, 1938.

7. *Lutherans and Catholics in Dialogue: III. The Eucharist as Sacrifice*, 1967.

8. *Ibid.*, pp. 89 ff.

9. Lumen Gentium, 2-17. Cf. *Sacrasanctum Concilium*, 2, 5-9.

10. Cf. Oscar Cullmann, *Christ and Time*, Philadelphia: Westminster Press, 1950.

11. *Lumen Gentium*, 9-17.

12. K. E. Skydsgaard in *Dialogue on the Way*, edited by George A. Lindbeck, Minneapolis: Augsburg Publishing House, 1965. pp. 145 ff.

13. Paul Minear, *Faith and Order Findings*, Minneapolis: Augsburg Publishing House, 1963.

14. *Verbum Dei*, esp. 17-20.

15. Paul Minear, *op. cit.*

16. *Ibid.*

17. *Ad Gentes.* Cf. the theological work of the Conferences on Life and Work and the Missionary Conference at Madras, India.

18. *Dignitatis Humanae.*

19. *Lumen Gentium,* 52-69. Cf. also René Laurentin, *Mary's Place in the Church,* London: Burns and Oates, 1965.

20. *Lumen Gentium,* 18-29.

21. Jacques Maritain, *The Peasant of the Garonne,* New York: Holt, Rinehart and Winston, 1968.

22. Decree on Ecumenism. Cf. the numerous statements by leaders of the ecumenical movement abjuring a super-church or unity based on uniformity or homogenization.

Chapter 5

Church, Unity, and History

There are enough surveys of the Christian efforts toward unity in the 20th century. A further survey is not to be added to their number. Rather the attempt will be made to analyze critically the present situation of the separated churches and their efforts toward unity in the light of previous developments and to sketch possible steps for the future. Certain aspects belonging necessarily to this theme can be omitted or mentioned only in passing as they are dealt with at length in other articles of this volume. This applies above all to the entrance of the Roman Catholic Church into the ecumenical movement and to the relation of the unity of the church and the unity of mankind.

THE HISTORICAL DIMENSION

The contradiction between unity and division is an element of the nature of the church of Jesus Christ. This statement goes beyond the confession that unity is one of the elements of the church's essence. Indeed, it contradicts it. But it is precisely here that the problem lies. The depth of this problem is not seen where the confession to the one church is confronted with the phenomenological fact of a divided Christendom. It is given a false perspective where a Platonic ideal of the one church willed by Christ and given in him is compared with the insufficient, partial realization of this ideal in history. In both cases the historical reality of the church is

144

not taken seriously. To distinguish and separate this reality from an ideal form, as if it were a pre-historical model, is to depreciate it.

In the first place, we can speak of the church of Jesus Christ only as a historical reality. That means that the confession to its unity as well as the contradiction between unity and division can be historically proved and demonstrated. Both, lying on the same level, are closely related. That, of course, cannot be deduced from the mere fact of a historically determined simultaneousness. Such statements, rather, are only possible in the dimension of God, the Creator and Sustainer, who revealed himself in history and is its judging and upholding Lord; in the dimension of Jesus Christ, who through his death and resurrection and rule over all powers transformed our history; and in the dimension of the Holy Spirit, who strengthens, leads, renews mankind on its way through history. In this historical action of the triune God, the church has its place. There is no other church, outside or behind this historical reality. The church set in this history is also the church of faith, for the special quality of this history is recognizable and acceptable only to faith.

That, however, is only the one side. The revealed historical action of the triune God does not form a special history of salvation defined by clear-cut boundaries and moving in parallel to secular history. Much rather it forms and penetrates a history which stands under the hidden rule of God, which is determined by the signs, existence, and active powers of God-estrangement, indifference, enmity, sin, and provisionality. In the introduction to this volume, this inseparable and not clearly distinguishable twofold determination of the one history was paraphrased with help of the two concepts "old history" and "new history." It is a history, which is ambiguous but at the same time dynamic, centered in itself and open for God's future.

It is in the midst of this history that the church lives. In the church the intimate connection and reciprocal penetration of "old" and "new" history reaches its sharpest, most evident and unresolvable historical concretion. It is the new mankind, which is reconciled through Jesus Christ with God and with one another. At the same time it bears within it the strongest denial of its being and its destination, because in it remain human weakness, blindness, narrowness, self-assertion, and will to power — and thus disobedience and sin toward God.

The Christological perspective of divine and human, applied to the church bypasses the historical reality of the church.[7] This holds true also for the concept of the church as the "extension" of the incarnation especially in the Anglican tradition, the reoccurring distinction between the visible and the invisible church in the Protestant tradition, and the identification of the church with the Body of Christ and the related doctrine of the sinlessness of the church (as opposed to the sinfulness of its members) in the Roman Catholic tradition. They are all based, consciously or unconsciously, on a double concept of the church, which in the last analysis is Platonic or Docetic. They are therefore unable to adequately deal with either the unity or the division of the church. They must either negate the factual division (there is only a division *from*, not *in* the church), or they must assign the unity and the division respectively to the invisible and visible church or to its divine and human side (which contradicts the Christological analogy).

It is more accurate, if an analogy is to be used at all, to characterize the church with help of the anthropological category of justified and at the same time sinner (*simul justus et peccator*). As we are dealing here with a statement of faith rooted in the midst of historical reality, so a separation between that which faith confesses about the church and the church's historical reality is also impossible. The consequence of being forced to deal only with this one reality is in no way a passive acceptance of the actual status quo of the church, now that the critical function of an ideal state is lacking. Rather the tension and contradiction between the historical destination of the church to be the one, holy, catholic and apostolic fellowship of the freed and reconciled, and its falling short of this destination are seen here in their real depth and intensity. They can no longer be assigned to two different spheres, which would make it possible to preserve the ideal.

If the church of Jesus Christ can be understood in faith as the focal point of the opposing powers and influences of the "old" and "new" history, then one must also speak of its essential destination of unity and of unity and division as elements of its nature. Both constitute its reality and at the same time qualify this reality as contradictory. Because the church lives at the center of a complex, ambiguous, contradictory history, this ambivalence and contradiction is manifested in the contradiction between unity and division. This contradiction will remain as long as the people of God are on their pilgrimage through history.

The contradictory sentence of the confession to the essential unity of the church, and of unity and division as elements of the nature of the church, which is held together by God and not only by the historical reality of the church, needs further clarification. A more detailed presentation is, however, not possible here. The unity of the church has its historical basis in the reconciling action of Jesus Christ. He has broken down the wall of separation between God and man and the many partitions between men. In this event, not only is the existence of the church grounded but also its unity. If unity is rightly understood, then reconciliation and unity, if not identical, are inseparably connected. He who has received and accepted the gift of reconciliation with God and refuses to be reconciled with his brother repudiates the gift of divine grace. It follows from this, that wherever the reconciling act of Jesus Christ is accepted by Word and Sacrament and finds expression in life and action, there the church of Jesus Christ *and its unity* is a historical reality. This is the case across all the boundaries which characterize the image of Christianity.

The last sentence could lead again to a double concept of the church, this time set in historical reality itself, as if there were a realization of the one church of Jesus Christ cutting across all confessions, from which the secondary organizational forms of the individual churches were to be distinguished. Church history bears witness to the repeated attempt to give the one church of Jesus Christ historical expression below or above the confessions and denominations (e.g., Zinzendorf, Disciples of Christ in the United States, and the Plymouth Brethren in Ireland and Great Britain. In some sense the present-day emigration of "progressive Christians" from the organized churches in the form of "secular-ecumenism" also belongs to this context). These attempts were extremely unhistorical, they ended in the formation of new fellowships and confessions and so only increased the divisions of Christianity. They showed in the last analysis, that an emigration of Christians from the tense, ambivalent and complex history in which God has placed them is not possible.

Precisely this nature of the history in which the church lives is the reason that the historical reality of the church's unity is concealed and thwarted by divisions, arising from different motives and origins. The unity can be concealed by distinctions and divisions of only superficial nature. It can be thwarted by divisions, in which truth stands against error, the struggle for discipleship against obdurate disobedience, the bold search for renewal open to the future against a lifeless orthodoxy in doctrine and institution cemented in the formulas of the past. On the other hand, the reality of unity will become recognizable and manifest in new historical expressions. It will gain scope and intensity as we are experiencing it in this century. But it will always be accompanied by separation and division, even by new divisions as long as the church lives in this world and history with all its ambiguity, peril, and provisionality.

Thus the church lives by the patient grace of God, who keeps his promise, who does not let the sinner fall, and who is at work in and through a divided Christianity. This work of the triune God in history and in a divided Christianity does not legitimize the status quo. It is a dynamic pushing forward of history toward its goal. Even now God is judging indirectly and directly the denials of his deed and his will. He allows a Christian fellowship which has become sterile and insipid to break apart and lets new signs of his coming and his reconciliation arise out of its ruins or beyond its previous bounds.

Against this background it becomes clearer how the confession to the unity of the church, its historical reality, and the reality of the division inseparable from it, are to be understood as elements of the nature of the church. This one historical reality is held together by God in a mysterious way, as he also holds together the divergent and contrary powers of the "old" and "new" histories. It cannot be resolved by man, but by God alone in the consummation of his kingdom. It is a dynamic, teleological reality, in which reconciliation is to gain scope over dissension and enmity. Here, too, men are called to be co-workers, instruments, "hands" of God and to give place to his grace and reconciliation, rather than selfishly cling to it or even suppress it. Here lies the unavoidable necessity for the churches to struggle ever anew to realize their true being and thus their unity. This can take place in the assurance that only in this way the divine judgment can become a saving judgment, and it must take place without the illusion or attempt, doomed from the start, of being able to achieve or complete it alone.

THE ECUMENICAL MOVEMENT – OUTLINES OF AN ANALYSIS

The approach to an understanding of the church, its unity and its divisions just sketched has certain implications for an analysis of the modern ecumenical movement and for possible steps into the future. Let us ask first of all about the implications for an analysis.

In view of the complex character of the modern ecumenical movement the historian and exegete endeavors to draw out certain basic lines, stages, and changes of this movement. Many examples of this can be given: 1) the distinction between the three great streams (missionary – theological – practical) and their union in the World Council of Churches (Faith and Order and Life and Work) and finally in New Delhi 1961 (World Council and International Missionary Council); 2) the distinction between an "erasmian," pietistic, and churchly ecumenism (Visser 't Hooft),[2] or an individual, churchly, and finally secular ecumenism (van den Heuvel),[3] or a first, second, and third ecumenical movement (document of Danish theologians)[4]; 3) within the "Movement for Life and Work" in the thirties, a stronger concern for theology and church can be observed;[5] 4) within the "Movement for Faith and Order" in the forties and fifties, a shift from a comparative ecclesiology to a concentration on the common center of faith and of the church;[6] 5) within the missionary thought and action of recent years, the increasing prominence of the concept of the missio Dei to the whole world over against more traditional concepts of mission;[7] 6) within the whole World Council the "discovery" of the eschatological dimension in the fifties,[8] the first outline of a picture of unity in New Delhi in 1961;[9] the ever stronger organizational, operational, and spiritual expansion of the ecumenical movement and of the World Council.

Clarifications and interpretations of this kind are necessary and to the point. Nevertheless, many of them seem to me to run the danger of over-simplification, of a too pronounced isolation of the ecumenical movement from the general developments in church and theology, and of not going deeply enough. The reason lies, I think, in a too exclusive concentration either on the organizational development of the ecumenical movement or on the various theological statements made within the frame of this movement. A closer look shows that the "ecumenical pioneers" are often understood as "creative personalities" detached from the historical context influencing them; that the thesis of a "churchly ecumenism" is valid in view of the organizational and representational forms of the World Council, but certainly not as valid in view of the historical reality of the churches themselves; that the reformulation of the task of mission is the work of only a minority; and that "secular ecumenism" in many respects is a new version of "erasmian" and pietistic ecumenism.

There can be no doubt that the rise of ecumenism within Christianity in this century has its impulses and origins in that comprehensive and complex history spoken of in the first chapter. It was certainly not a discovery or rediscovery of the biblically proclaimed gift and therefore our task of unity in the realm of theology, which gave rise to the movement for Faith and Order. The texts from the first phase of this movement (1910-1920) show clearly that it was a new historical situation from which the challenge and the call to unity was recognized and accepted.[10] What has previously been accepted as constitutive for the movement toward unity in the area of mission (since Edinburgh 1910) and of "Life and Work" (since the preparatory conference in Champel 1920 and the World Conference in Stockholm 1925) — the changed historical situation with its upheavals, new dangers, problems, tasks, and possibilities — applies also to the movement in theology to overcome the divisions in doctrine and order of the churches. The entry of the first Orthodox churches into the ecumenical movement was also essentially occasioned by the changed historical situation after the First World War.[11] The significance of the great "ecumenical pioneers" in the first decades is that they possessed a special sensitivity for the challenges posed to Christianity by history. They reflected upon these challenges, articulated them, and transformed them into plans, conceptions, organizations, hopes, and prayers.

We must first of all emphasize the deep rooting of the ecumenical movement in that comprehensive and dynamic history of God with his world, which encompasses the action of a hidden and revealing God as well as the deeds of an obedient, sinful, and ignorant mankind. Only from this starting point is it legitimate to speak of an action of God, of a guidance of the Holy Spirit in view of the ecumenical movement. In this movement is manifest the divine dynamic of history in which reconciliation is to gain scope among Christians, the churches, and all men. And yet, it is not possible to simply equate the ecumenical movement with an aspect of the history of salvation, for at the same time the ambiguous and contradictory character belonging to all history and all historical movements is manifest in it. Here lies the deep justification of all criticisms of the failure, shortcomings, and one-sidedness of the ecumenical endeavor. Here too the "Yes" is genuine only together with the "No," yet both must be embraced by the knowledge of the provisional character and open future of this historical movement.

Out of this basic rooting of the ecumenical movement in history arise further inferences for an analysis of the ecumenical movement. We must concentrate here on two basic aspects. The *first* concerns the significance of the so-called "non-theological factors" for the divisions and the unity of Christianity. This question has received increasing attention since about 1935.[12] As a methodological tool, the distinction between theological and non-theological factors can be possible and helpful. It can clarify the problem of division and unity, but contributes little to its solution as it easily leads to wrong conclusions. This distinction implies in most cases a qualitative judgment. Accordingly, only the deeper theological differences or similarities are of final importance. The historical implications of the social, political, national, economical, racial, and cultural causes of many divisions — as also of many efforts toward unity — are indeed seen and, where religiously disguised, demasked. But they finally serve only the analysis, a kind of "ecumenical psychoanalysis" which already promises healing. They are not made an object of theological reflection, and because they are only "non-theological" and thus secondary, they are to have no decisive importance for the unity and division, but are to be relativized or overcome.

Already the factual experience of the churches shows that this is a wrong conclusion. This understanding also blocks a proper theological approach to the fact that "non-theological" differences often prove stronger and more influential than far-reaching theological agreements. If one, however, proceeds from the comprehensive, complex historical reality in which the church of Jesus Christ lives and in which it participates, then another perspective opens up. It is still possible to distinguish between theological (in the narrow sense) and non-theological factors, but not to separate them. I would even say that in the strict sense of the word, one should no longer speak of "non-theological" factors in connection with the problem of unity and division. There are two reasons for this. First, cultural, social, political, ideological, ethnic, economic, and other elements of history not only exercise a manifold influence on the theological and ecclesiastical movements, but also enter into them, they are of eminent theological importance. Of course, these movements must be interpretations of the biblical witness, in critical reception of its historical transmission. And yet they can only take place within the actual context of history, regardless of how they react to it, and in anticipation of the leading of the Holy Spirit. There is, therefore, no theological or ecclesiological decision which could be separated from these factors without becoming abstract, unhistorical, and thus irrelevant and ineffectual.

Secondly, these factors and elements are theologically relevant already in that they are components of the dynamic, onward-pressing history of God. They must be evaluated theologically as to their significance in assisting or hindering the reconciling action of the triune God. It is too often overlooked that racial discrimination does not become theologically relevant in the effect it has upon a Christian fellowship gathered around Word and Sacrament or upon the relation of several Christian communities to each other. Racial discrimination as such is to be qualified theologically as disobedience and sin because it denies the reconciling deed of Jesus Christ in history and contradicts his continuing reconciling action through the Holy Spirit. Is this cause of divisions theologically less significant and historically less effective before God and man than a divergent understanding of the presence of Christ in the Lord's Supper?

Such an understanding requires a more comprehensive theological perspective, also in viewing the ecumenical movement. It was indicated that the origins of the modern ecumenical movement lie outside the theological realm as such. That can now no longer mean that this movement has a non-theological origin. We are rather now, following the discussion of the non-theological factors, in the position to repeat and underscore the statement, that it has its origin in the history of God with this world. This thesis need not be explained again. Proceeding from this basic statement, differentiations and clarifications are now possible and necessary.

We thus come to a *second* inference from the historical rooting of the ecumenical movement. Although theology and history, including the history of the church, are inseparably related, attention must now be directed to the *relation between theology in the narrower sense and its historical context*.

It becomes evident here that the movement for Faith and Order was a reaction to the historical challenge, which was directly oriented toward theology and the church. In the movement for Life and Work and in the efforts toward unity in the realm of missions, the theological reaction set in only later and more gradually. Here the actual, practical questions stood in the foreground from the very beginning. This theological reaction in these movements took the form of a common reflection that aimed from the very start at historical relevancy. The challenge posed by the world and history was understood as a reminder and call to obedience toward the prayer and command of Christ that all should be one. The possibilities of following this call were discussed with the one aim that this reflection should open the way for concrete steps of the churches.

One can thus speak of an interrelation between a reaction to history, and, proceeding from this reaction and reflection, an action with the goal of moving history forward. It should not be overlooked that this theological reaction and reflection should be a *critical* one whose intended historical effects and consequences must be oriented to the future. Furthermore in consciously entering the ambiguous and open realm of history, it runs the risk of error and failure.

The interrelation between theological reaction and reflection on the one hand, and history on the other, has found different expressions in the modern ecumenical movement. But at times it has also been wholly neglected or disfigured — and it is precisely here that the real causes for the weaknesses, one-sidednesses, and fictions of this movement are to be sought. Three examples will make this clear. We begin once again with the first period of *"Faith and Order"* after 1910. Faith and Order was a genuine theological reaction to the special, changed situation of the times before and after the First World War. The theological reflection on the unity of the church, which arose out of that situation, did not take place within the theological field in the narrow sense. Rather, it included the historical point of departure in its reflection. That is evident in the fact that the question of the unity of mankind was expressly taken up into the context of the search for the unity of the churches.

There were also theological attempts, typical for that time, to understand the unity of the church as an instrument in the sense of a Christianization of the social and cultural structures of the world. It is significant that here the historical locus of the church was recognized and thus also the necessity for the interrelation between theology and history. The danger of conceiving the unity of the church as an end in itself was thus avoided. But it was not avoided at the point where the search for unity among Christians took on the defensive character of a strong, unified front against non-Christian or anti-Christian movements in the first half of the 20th century. Of course, that interrelation is present here too. It is, however, qualitatively a quite different kind.[13]

That the historical consequences of this theological reflection were so insignificant is to be explained by the still strongly individual character of the ecumenical movement in its first two or three decades. This does not mean to confirm the thesis that an individualistic understanding of church unity was dominant in the first phase of this movement — that was certainly not the case. Rather, this phase was shaped by single persons, for whom the possibilities for far-reaching actions were of different kinds and in most cases limited. That is what made up its individual character.

There is, however, still another reason for its ineffectiveness, and that brings us directly back to our starting point. The theological reaction and reflection in Faith and Order isolated itself from that total historical context, to which it owed its origin. This meant that now individual, isolated points of theological controversy such as grace, church, sacraments, ministry, and church unity were put into the center of the common theological effort. This led to a neglect of the actual developments taking place within church and theology — e.g., the church union efforts and the rise of dialectical theology in the 1920s and 1930s, or the break-through of the modern historical-critical exegesis and the revival of a conservative-evangelical church life and theology after the Second World War. The wider and more comprehensive area of profane history was either assigned to "Life and Work" or was neutralized in the form of "non-theological factors" as a special section or appendix of Faith and Order.

There is no question that Faith and Order performed significant theological work before and after the Second World War. It is just as clear that the insignificant historical effectiveness of this work is the result of the insufficient attention given to the historical reality of the church and of the world. This also expresses a certain schematic view. Therefore, it must be acknowledged that the introduction of the question of intercommunion and of worship (Lund, 1952),[14] the preparation of the statement on unity (New Delhi, 1961),[15] the treatment of the problems of institution and tradition (Montreal, 1963),[16] the study on "God in Nature and History,"[17] the attention paid to the union negotiations in recent years, and the current studies on ordination, intercommunion, and on the unity of the church and the unity of mankind — to name but a few — signal the return to a more comprehensive historical dimension of the work of Faith and Order. This return does not guarantee historical consequences, but can make it more likely through a stronger connection between history and theological reflection.

Also in the second great line of the ecumenical movement, *Life and Work*, the interrelation between theological reaction and reflection on the one hand, and history on the other, has undergone a significant development. It was not until Oxford 1937 and Amsterdam 1948 that the theological reaction to the historical challenge reached a greater depth and, in the conception of the "responsible society," the possibility of creative historical influence.[18] After 1948, theological reflection in this field had to yield priority to practical cooperation of the churches. Some isolated attempts were made, in the study on "Rapid Social Change," [19] to maintain "theological contact" to the developments in the world.

However, the Geneva World Conference on Church and Society in 1966 made it all too clear how ill prepared one was theologically for the new historical challenges of our time.[20] That was true not only of reflection in the realm of social ethics within the World Council, but also of Faith and Order. The strict departmentalization between social ethics and dogmatics proved to be impossible, as questions of an understanding of God and revelation become of fundamental importance in the social ethics discussion. In order to catch up with these new developments, present theological work within the ecumenical institutions is concentrating on reaction and reflection in view of the new situation. Examples of this are the Fourth Assembly of the WCC in Uppsala and the new studies on the "Humanum," which have been taken up by different units within the WCC.[21]

Through the new situation, to which theology reacted relatively late, the interrelation between theology and history has entered a new crucial test, which is already understood by many people as a crisis of the institutionalized ecumenical movement. This crisis reaches far into the life and thought of many churches themselves. One could describe this crisis, which is understood by others as a turning point to a "third ecumenical movement" [22] along the following lines: to the new historical challenges — racial discrimination, social injustice, and revolutionary revolt against the power of the rich and of the ruling classes, inequality between the rich North and the poor South of the world and so the necessity of development and worldwide economic justice, the problems of peace, of hunger, and of the control of new, technocratic power structures, the questioning of traditions, institutions, and authority, and much more — many groups of Christians seek an answer in social engagement and in new forms of fellowship and service within and outside the churches.

We can discuss these very different undertakings here only insofar as they have relevance for the ecumenical movement. One of the marks of these groups is that they are as a rule inter-denominational. They experience a deep unity in common service which leads them to feel that the ecumenical effort to overcome the traditional differences in doctrine between the churches is a worn out matter. They draw a position outside the institutionalized ecumenical movement and practice their own "secular ecumenism." [23] This ecumenism is certainly more than just a direct continuation of the old "Life and Work" tendencies. It presents a challenge to the churchly and ecumenical institutions. Whether it represents a "turning-point" is doubtful in view of the many parallels to the unhistorical, individual, pietistic forms of the early ecumenical movement.

The World Council of Churches has attempted not without some success to catch up with the advance guard of "secular ecumenism." [24] It has therefore, made itself suspect among the evangelical wing of Christianity, which has always viewed it with reserve or rejection, for giving preference to a certain theological-social ethical party line. In addition, the majority of member churches, which are by no means only conservative in thought, increasingly make the reproach that the reflective theological reactions to the challenges of the times have not always been comprehensive and deep enough. This reproach can also be made of the churches.

That attempts have been made in the World Council since Uppsala to move on to a deeper and more comprehensive theological reflection is also obvious.[25] This reflection includes the dilemma just mentioned in which the ecumenical movement finds itself at the present. Otherwise it would remain partial, bypassing history and losing the possibility of becoming historically effective. In other words, the question is raised today with an urgency hitherto unknown, not only whether the placing of the church in history can be taken seriously theologically, but whether it can theologically — and that must always mean historically — be mastered, in view of the tremendous polarizations in the world and in Christianity and in view of the widespread uncertainty about the future of both.

We choose still a third example as illustrative of the problem of the interrelation between theology and history in the context of the ecumenical movement. This time it has to do with the World Council of Churches itself. It must be said here on the positive side that already at its First Assembly in Amsterdam in 1948, the report of Section I acknowledged and articulated the broader historical dimension of the church. In this manner, the differing doctrines of the churches were seen in the deeper context of the wholeness of the life and history of the churches.[26] The Assembly at Uppsala, twenty years later, went a step further. It formulated under the key word "catholicity" basic lines of a view of the church and of the fellowship of the churches which is universal and comprehensive.[27]

I think that here a way was shown for overcoming the distinction between the so-called theological and non-theological factors which was methodologically in part necessary but materially dangerous. With this an essential basis was created for future theological work in which the interrelation between theology and history can be held together more closely than before. With this understanding of catholicity, the theological task outlined above would have a greater chance of being realized.

Here too, however, critical remarks must be made. The World Council of Churches is a historically determined entity which claims both to represent and to shape history. Here, too, we find an interrelation. The responsive and reflective element is to be found in the practical and theological work done by the World Council, and also in the reflection on its (instrumental) significance and task, even on its ecclesiological significance.[28] The historical-creative element, on the other hand, is less easy to define. Without doubt, much that takes place today in the common service of Christians in the world and much that has changed in the relation of the churches among themselves, would scarcely have been possible without the fact of the World Council. On the other hand, one observes that many churches or Christian communities and groups are either touched little or not at all by the work and thought within the World Council, or that they develop new structures of ecumenical thought and action outside the ecumenical institutions.

That is true for groups on the left, the right, and for churches and groups in the middle of the total spectrum of Christian theory, practice, and institutions. The reasons for this are doubtlessly to be sought on both sides. We are interested here in some of the possible reasons on the side of the World Council. How is it possible, that a constantly growing quantitative churchly representation in the World Council, and an increasing reflection on its ecclesiological significance has produced such a relatively weak historical resonance in the churches? Is the thesis of a second, "churchly" phase of the ecumenical movement just a fiction, or at most only an imperfectly realized ideal?

It has to do essentially with the problem of representation. The historical reality of the churches, which is the foundation and goal of all reflection and action of the World Council, is only formally and partially represented in its structures. It is only formally represented, because the decisive organs in the World Council are constituted in a way in which the people of God in all the world are scarcely better represented than the Roman Catholic Church by its Council of Bishops. This also touches upon the problem of a structure of representation based on confession and numerical strength. The historical reality is also only partially represented. Some reasons for this are: 1) the predominance of western thought forms and conceptions in view of the situation of the Christians in the "third world"; 2) the control of finances which makes a certain selection of participants for consultations and conferences possible; 3) the formation of an ecumenical "in-group" centered around an "ecumenical technocracy," a group which sets priorities for ecumenical action and thought based on its specific experiences and presuppositions; 4) the insufficient consideration given to the "conservative" groups and interests within Christianity; and 5) the rise of an ecumenical bureaucracy out of touch with reality.

It would be unjust not to acknowledge that these dangers and deficiencies are seen in the ecumenical institutions and that ways are being sought to overcome them.[29] The question is whether the institutions are flexible enough to allow far-reaching changes in their structures. At the moment this is doubtful. It is clear that the problem of representation (and directly connected with it that of institution), is of decisive importance for the "functioning" of the interrelation of theological reflection and theologically based action on the one hand and history on the other. The insufficient representation of the total history of church and world in the World Council of Churches is certainly one of the main reasons for its limited historical effectiveness. It must be finally emphasized that a more comprehensive representation, which must be demanded as one of the presuppositions for a greater historical effectiveness, must not be confused or identified with an indifferent acceptance of all that claims historical reality today in church and world. We will deal with this question again later on.

In this second part of the paper the attempt was made to draw some basic lines for the analysis of the modern ecumenical movement, for an analysis which views more comprehensively the historical dimension of the problem of division and unity. Two remarks are still necessary here. First, these basic lines for analysis are not solidly established because they could not be developed and justified in detail in this paper. But even a detailed analysis would not be able to reach final, uncontradictable results. For precisely when an analysis includes the historical dimension in this way, i.e., a dimension not characterized by unequivocalness and finality, it can offer no more than a description of the very complex historical character of the ecumenical movement which resists being pressed into a fixed scheme. But such a description is precisely what we lack!

Second, the objection could be raised that the criteria used here (such as theological/non-theological factors; interrelation between theological reaction/reflection and history) once again press historical reality into a scheme. I have sought to take these criteria from history itself. But there is no question that these alone are insufficient for a detailed analysis and must be supplemented by others. Such a further criterion would be, for example, the significance of the past and the future for the problem of the division and unity of the church. An analysis of the ecumenical movement undertaken from this viewpoint would lead to further differentiated results. We will make use of this criterion at the end of the final part of this paper.

ECUMENICAL PERSPECTIVES

An analysis of the ecumenical movement is not a game *l'art pour l'art*. It is only meaningful when it sheds light on the present situation and shows possibilities for the future path. We cannot look back as spectators upon a movement in which we ourselves are still involved. When I said that the analysis can show possibilities for the future path a warning was necessary. Because we have to do with a movement, with a historical reality which has proved to be stronger than all institutional attempts to contain it, we must expect that much will develop in the future differently than we expected or planned. When history in the broadest sense stands under the rule and guidance of God and is at the same time shaped by men who acknowledge this rule and guidance only in the conflict of obedience and disobedience, then two conclusions can be drawn. We cannot dispensate ourselves from planning and shaping the future, because as God's co-workers we are responsible to him and to our fellow man. This cooperation comprehends the risk of error and failure as well as the certainty of forgiveness. In the second place, it comprehends that God shows more imagination in directing his world and history than we ever dream. We have the future in our hands — we do not have the future in our hands. There is nothing left for us but to recognize and realize the first statement in the dimension of the second. Is there a more realistic perspective for the future of the search for unity among Christians?

We think that the qualitative understanding of catholicity offers possibilities for progress in the search for unity among Christians in the total dimension of history. The new conception of catholicity fulfills a basic critical function. That is spelled out already in the Uppsala report.[30] We are interested in the creative function of this conception and in the reality meant by it. This conception should serve to place in a larger context the extremely diverse historical conditions and expressions of the present unity, of the existing divisions, of the search for unity, and of the denials of and obstacles to this search. From this perspective creative steps into the future would possess a greater relevancy for the whole ecumenical movement. The present proposal of a truly universal council as a possible form of reaching this goal is no patent solution.[31] Apart from the necessity of concrete plans for such an event, it would require certain presuppositions. It must avoid being burdened with the deficiencies of the present mechanisms for representation in churchly and ecumenical institutions.

We want to deal here with one of these presuppositions. First of all, everything must be done to prevent the different and often contrary powers and tendencies within the churches and within the ecumenical movement from breaking apart by bringing them into relationship. That is a matter of good will, not of indifference. It makes a theological conception and historical structures necessary.

One could designate one of the deepest controversies within present Christianity as that between the insistence upon an "orthodox thought" and the insistence upon an "orthodox practice." This controversy has far-reaching consequences for the present ecumenical movement. Were it a mere controversy between "doctrine" and "action," then a kind of "peaceful coexistence" could perhaps be quickly reached. The difficulty lies precisely in the fact that "orthodox thought" leads to a certain action and that "orthodox action" presupposes a certain doctrine or theory. At the same time this difficulty offers a chance that has scarcely been recognized. Both sides of this controversy thus have certain points in common. That is a statement of fact. How can these common points be understood so that a genuine relationship can be developed from them?

When the new conception of catholicity includes both the overcoming of the difference between theological and non-theological factors and the interrelation between theology in the narrow sense and history in the widest sense, then both sides of the controversy can be seen in a new light. One result of this could be that each side puts questions to the other on the basis of these two criteria. The side of "orthodox thought," which emphasizes God's revelation in the life, death, and resurrection of Christ; the proclamation of the gospel, the administration of the sacraments; and the work of the Holy Spirit in creating the answer of faith, must allow the question if it is conscious of the historical character of faith and of the church. In other words, whether it realizes that it has all too often succumbed to the temptation of dissociating faith and the church from the total historical dimension. Has this side, which put so much emphasis upon "orthodoxy," not in fact often become heretical in its silence to or conformity with historical movements, developments, and tendencies — when "heresy" is not only understood as the departure from pure doctrine, but also departure from proper practice? Examples of this are well known. Must this side not come to the conviction, that "orthodox thought" without "orthodox action" is an unsuccessful attempt to escape out of the history of God with his world and mankind?

The side of "orthodox action," which emphasizes the service and involvement of Christians together with all men of good will in the social structures of this world in order to change these structures, must allow the question, whether or not it is conscious of the historical character of its action. In other words, does it realize that through the creative and sustaining work of God and through the inauguration of a new mankind reconciled with God and one another in Jesus Christ, history has been given not only a forward moving drive, but also an ambivalence within which Christian action finds its basis only in the "new history" of God and in expectation of its consummation? Must not "orthodox action" heed the warning of "orthodox thought" — that the loss of a basis of historical action means to fall prey to an activism, which holds the fiction that history and its future are unambiguous? "Orthodox action" must not lose the capability of criticizing its own actions.

These are only some suggestions for a possible relationship between two basic positions, whose conflict is in part responsible for the present crisis in the churches and in the ecumenical movement. It has to do with a relationship in the form of a dialog in which each side questions and challenges the other. This means a dialog which dares not remain only verbal, but should lead on both sides to changes, to greater openness, corrections, and a wider perspective; a dialog which should be the instrument and expression of genuine catholicity.

This dialog requires at least two presuppositions. Both sides must be prepared to participate, and structures must be created for it. It cannot simply be said that the prior willingness to enter into dialog must lead to the creation of structures. It could be that suitable structures would waken and support this willingness. The willingness to enter into this dialog could arise at the point where the unfathomable richness of the will and action of God and the broad scope of human answers to this richness is acknowledged. This includes the willingness to concede the possibility of error on one's side as well as the possibility of the recognition and realization of truth on the other side.

This willingness and openness is limited only at the point where the one or the other side considers itself absolute, or, in maintaining its absoluteness damns the other side; or where one side explicitly or implicitly denies the centrality of the "new history" of God revealed and become universal in the saving event of Jesus Christ. I believe that within these bounds, a dialog could lead to a new, dynamic, and creative fellowship of differing positions.

The structures which could initiate or make possible such a dialog in the ecumenical realm are for the most part lacking. Here we come back to what was said earlier about representation. That means that the present ecumenical structures at all levels which serve either the dialog between the different confessions or the dialog within an often one-sidedly constituted ecumenical "in-group" must be changed, expanded, supplemented, and made more open and dynamic in such a way that they make possible a more comprehensive representation of the different positions, groups, and tendencies in Christianity. Representation, not in a static or statistical form, but in the sense and in the interest of encounter and of dialog. Only when the ecumenical movement gains a catholicity in this sense does it have a future. Only in the presupposition of this form of catholicity can the hope placed in a truly universal council become a concrete hope.

Genuine catholicity is only possible in the dimension of divine and human reconciliation. The new dialog in the structures of a more comprehensive representation as sketched here, as well as the already existing dialog between the separated churches, can and must be understood and undertaken only as an instrument of this reconciliation in dependence upon the work of the Holy Spirit. In the simultaneousness and intended convergence within both dialogs as well as between them, the one, new mankind, reconciled with God and with one another, can gain a more visible and historically more effective expression. The unity of Christians in this historical context cannot be a repristination of an earlier condition, cannot be a "re-union." This attempt and idea is all too familiar and too often used in the ecumenical movement. It would not only be a fiction, but would contradict the history of God which is directed at the future and at change.

The process of reconciliation and therefore of union is a process of change, renewal, and hope. It has its roots in the past, which has so shaped us and torn us apart that we are led to recognize the need of reconciliation. It must be continued further in the present by coming to terms with our denominational and confessional past, in the reconciling dialog between different and contrary positions, in the prophetic concretion which from the freedom granted in Jesus Christ challenges static institutions and one-sided orthodoxies of thought and action, drawing them beyond themselves into a search for a new convergence. This is to be a convergence which no longer sees its goal in the attempt to formulate a theological consensus, but in a mutual acknowledgement of multiple expressions of doctrine, life, and action.

It will remain the task of an ecumenical theology to outline the possible structures and bounds of such a diversity in the convergent movement of Christian thought and action.[32] The process of reconciliation is directed at the future, for the reconciliation and unity of Christians, and through them of all mankind, is not a matter that finds fulfillment in a particular point in history. It is rather imbedded in the dynamic and ambivalence of the total history of God with his world. We can, therefore, never be satisfied and take our rest in the preliminary and imperfect accomplishments of the moment, but must stride forward in the expectation that the Lord of all history will bring his pilgrim people, whom he accompanies on their way, to its goal. Then we will no longer need ecumenical perspectives.

— Translated by Donald Dutton

NOTES

1. Some traces of this idea are still recognizable in the official Report of the Lund Conference (cf. *A Documentary History of the Faith and Order Movement* 1927-1963, Lukas Vischer, ed., St. Louis, 1963, e.g. p. 88 and 91 f.), and in one of the preparatory documents for Montreal (cf. *Christ*

and the Church, Faith and Order Paper No. 38, p. 19 f. and 47-49, in
Faith and Order Findings, Paul S. Minear, ed., London, 1963.)

2. W. A. Visser 't Hooft, "Our Ecumenical Task in the Light of History,"
The Ecumenical Review, vol. VII, No. 4, 1955, p. 309 ff.

3. Albert van den Heuvel, "Toward a Secular Understanding of the Ecumenical?" In A. van den Heuvel, *The Humiliation of the Church,* London,
1967, p. 92 ff.

4. "The World Council of Churches and the Churches," IDOC research,
mimeographed, 1969, pp. 5-13.

5. This development reached its climax in the 1937 Oxford Conference on
"Church, Community and State" (a new Edition of the Report was pub-
lished under the title *Foundations of Ecumenical Social Thought,* ed. by
J. H. Oldham, Philadelphia, 1966), esp. p. 11 f.

6. This change occurred already before the Lund Conference of 1952 (there
are even voices in the thirties asking for a step beyond a mere comparison of the churches), yet the new approach is most clearly to be found
in the Report of a Theological Commission in preparation for Lund *(The
Church,* Faith and Order Papers No. 7, Geneva, 1951), and in the official
Lund Report *(The Third World Conference on Faith and Order held at
Lund,* August 15-28, 1952, Oliver S. Tomkins, ed., London, 1953, esp.
pp. 11-22).

7. This concept determined highly the Draft for Section II of the 1968
Uppsala Assembly ("Renewal in Mission," in *Drafts for Sections,* Geneva,
1968, p. 28 ff.). This draft was one of the most controversial Uppsala
documents.

8. Cf. the main addresses by Edmund Schlink in Lund ("The Pilgrim People
of God," in *The Third World Conference on Faith and Order,* p. 151 ff.),
and Evanston 1954 ("Christ — the Hope of the World," in *The Evanston
Report,* W. A. Visser 't Hooft, ed., New York, 1955), and the Reports of
the two Conferences *(The Third World Conference on Faith and Order,*
p. 19 ff.; *The Evanston Report,* Statement of the Assembly concerning
the Main Theme).

9. *The New Delhi Report,* W. A. Visser 't Hooft, ed., London, 1962, p. 116 ff.

10. Cf. The official, numbered Faith and Order Papers, Series 1, No. 1-32
(1910-1919).

11. The significant "Message of the Ecumenical Patriarchate" (1920) shows
this very clearly. A new translation of this Message can be found in
The Ecumenical Review, vol. XII, No. 1, Geneva, 1959, p. 79 ff.

12. One of the preparatory documents for the World Conference on Faith
and Order in Edinburgh 1937 dealt with this subject: *The Non-Theological
Factors in the Making and Unmaking of Church Union,* W. L. Sperry, ed.,
Faith and Order Papers No. 84, New York/London, 1937.

13. I have tried to prove this in a book on the concepts of unity in Faith and
Order which will be published in the near future.

14. Cf. the two preparatory volumes *Ways of Worship,* London, 1951, and
Intercommunion, London, 1952, and the Lund Section Reports on the
same themes.

15. Cf. "Report of the Commission on Faith and Order to the Central Committee on the Subject of the Future of Faith and Order," in *Minutes of the Faith and Order Commission 1960*, St. Andrews, Scotland. Faith and Order Paper No. 31, Geneva, 1960, pp. 28 ff., 97 ff., and 103.

16. *Faith and Order Findings*, including Faith and Order Paper No. 37 on "Institutionalism" and No. 40 on "Tradition and Traditions"; *The Fourth World Conference on Faith and Order*, P. C. Rodger and L. Vischer, ed., London, 1964, p. 50 ff.

17. *Study Encounter*, vol. I, No. 3, Geneva, 1965. *New Directions in Faith and Order* — Bristol 1967, Faith and Order Paper No. 50, Geneva, 1968, pp. 7 ff.

18. Especially in the Report of Section III of the Amsterdam Assembly (*The First Assembly of the World Council of Churches*, W. A. Visser 't Hooft, ed., London, 1949, p. 74 ff.

19. A summary of the Rapid Social Change Study 1955-1960 is to be found in *Evanston to New Delhi*, Report of the Central Committee to the Third Assembly of the World Council of Churches, Geneva, 1961, pp. 48 ff. and *The Ecumenical Advance. A History of the Ecumenical Movement*. vol. II, 1948-1968. Harold E. Fey, ed., London, 1970, pp. 274 ff.

20. World Conference on Church and Society, Official Report, Geneva, 1967. One of the highly critical commentaries to this Conference was written by Paul Ramsey, *Who Speaks for the Church?*, Nashville/New York, 1967. An attempt to take up the theological questions was made in the Report "*Theological Issues of Church and Society*," *Study Encounter*, vol. IV, No. 2, Geneva, 1968, pp. 70 ff.

21. *The Uppsala 68 Report*, Geneva, 1968, p. 202 ff.

22. Cf. the IDOC Document referred to in footnote No. 4.

23. Cf. the document "Secular Ecumenism," which was prepared by the Institute for Ecumenical Research, Strasbourg, for the Assembly of the Lutheran World Federation in Evian, 1970.

24. *Planning for Mission*, Thomas Wieser, ed., New York, 1966; *The Church for Others*, Geneva, 1967. A critical evaluation of the results of this study is presented by H. T. Neve, *Sources for Change. Searching for flexible church structures*, Geneva, 1968.

25. For example in the comprehensive study project on the "Humanum," cf. "Co-ordinated Studies on Man," *Study Encounter*, vol. IV, No. 3, Geneva, 1968, p. 122 ff. and The Uppsala 68 Report, p. 202 ff.

26. *The First Assembly of the World Council of Churches*, esp. pp. 52 and 55.

27. *The Uppsala 68 Report*, p. 11 ff.

28. Dr. Visser 't Hooft has repeatedly brought this question into the discussion. One of the earliest instances is his report on The Meaning of Membership in the WCC, in *Minutes and Reports of the Seventeenth Meeting of the Central Committee of the WCC*, Rochester, N.Y., USA, August 26-September 2, 1963. Geneva, 1964, p. 134 ff.

29. A "Structure Committee" of the WCC is working on these problems, cf. the "Report on the Re-examination of the Structure of the WCC from the

Central Committee to the Fourth Assembly" in *The Uppsala 68 Report*, p. 355 ff.

30. *The Uppsala 68 Report*, p. 14 f.

31. *The Uppsala 68 Report*, p. 16. Lukas Vischer, "A Genuinely Universal Council . . . ?" In *Central Committee of the WCC, Minutes and Reports of the Twenty-third Meeting*, Canterbury, August 12-22nd, 1969, Geneva, 1969, p. 182 ff.

32. Cf. the important and constructive outline by Edmund Schlink: "The Unity and Diversity of the Church," in Reinhard Groscurth, ed., *What Unity Implies. Six Essays After Uppsala*, p. 33 ff. See also Karl Rahner, "Pluralism in Theology and the Unity of the Church's Profession of Faith," in: *Concilium*, vol. 6, No. 5, 1969, p. 49 ff.

Chapter 6

Secular Ecumenism:
One Church—One World

Only ten years ago nobody thought of the ecumenical movement as anything but an intra-Christian or intra-church affair. Whether one considered ecumenism as the increasing of friendship between Christians of differing churches, the negotiations toward various church unions, or as the establishing of ecumenical agencies, all these aspects occurred within the boundary lines of the Christian church.

With the advent of secular ecumenism, the ecumenical movement spills out beyond the bounds of the church and into the secular, even non-Christian world. In the decade of the 1960s the term suddenly became a household word in ecumenical circles. Yet it is really an outgrowth of a theological reflection which has been simmering in the church for some time, and it is no exaggeration to predict that secular ecumenism is the hand-writing on the wall which promises that the future of ecumenism will be profoundly altered by these theological currents which give secular ecumenism its form and force.

On the surface, secular ecumenism

consists in collaboration among Christians in attempting to solve the baffling secular problems of our time such as racial injustice, poverty, and the blight of the slums.[1]

Christians from divided churches are increasingly being drawn together in the church's social ministry. Protestants and Roman Catholics work with each other and with others in inner-city missions, link arms in demonstrations against social and racial inequities, and establish joint youth clubs. This trend has also been termed "social ecumenism," "pastoral ecumenism," and "practical ecumenism."

At first glance, secular ecumenism is a growing unity in the church's service or mission. This is true, but this in itself is not particularly new or original. Decades ago "Life and Work" was launched in the conviction that "doctrine divides but service unites," and that the church's practical work should be done cooperatively. In the United States the Social Gospel movement also encouraged joint work in the social realm.

But a second glance in the following pages will make it quite clear that secular ecumenism is a new kind of ecumenical phenomenon. "Life and Work" understood itself as a unity of action running parallel to the doctrinal barriers which yet remained. Its perspective was, "We might be divided doctrinally, but apart from that we can at least work together." Secular ecumenism stands in direct contrast: it is solidly rooted in a theological outlook which takes as its starting point the church's existence in the secularized world and is convinced that the urgency of this challenge is itself an irresistible centripetal force toward unity which overshadows the doctrinal divisions of the past.

Nor can secular ecumenism be identified as a reincarnation of the Social Gospel movement. There may be enough similarities to justify labelling the Social Gospel a predecessor of secular ecumenism, but the theological climate of today is a far cry from the times of Walter Rauschenbusch and company.

The increasing involvement of the Christian church in current social problems and the growing cooperation among churches dealing with these problems is the outward manifestation of secular ecumenism.[2] What interests us here, however, are the theological developments in Roman Catholic and Lutheran thinking which stand behind this ecumenical thrust into the secular world. For ultimately secular ecumenism is more than practical cooperation among Christian churches in secular areas of human need: At its heart lies the conviction that the Christian mission (and therefore Christian action and unity as well) somehow encompasses the whole family of man, the whole secular world, the entire *oikumene*.[3] The key to understanding this phenomenon of secular ecumenism lies therefore in the word "secular," with which we begin this study.

SECULARIZATION AND THE CHURCH

The process of secularization has been creeping in upon us for a long time, but only since the Second World War has it emerged as a major topic of theological consideration. Within that time it has become obvious that the issues revolving around secularization have become predominant in the church's life.

A study of secularization itself would burst the limits of this essay. Our specific question is rather, how has secularization affected ecumenism?

One purely technological aspect might be mentioned briefly. In a world where news circles the globe in a split second, where man needs only a few hours to reach any metropolis in the world, and where the affairs of other continents appear daily on our television screens, no church can exist any longer in a comfortable ecclesiastical ghetto. Whatever our attitude to the ecumenical movement might be, we are compelled to rub shoulders with the world and with other churches by the sheer finesse of modern science.

But this aspect is only peripheral. The real answer to our question is indirect; secularization has caused a profound shift of our theological perspectives, and this shift in turn produces an entirely new outlook on ecumenism.

The most apparent mark of secularization is a world increasingly autonomous of churchly or "religious" reference. In the Middle Ages the church was the overarching social institution; kings and rulers consulted the bishops on foreign policy; theology reigned as queen of the sciences, and the clergy were respected as leading scholars in all fields of learning. From the time of the Renaissance these ecclesiastical privileges have been slowly eroded away, until now in the industrialized western world all aspects of human society — economic, political, social, technological, educational, etc. — operate relatively free from churchly oversight or religious reference. Some countries are more thoroughly "secular" than others where the religious social atmosphere still lingers, but who would doubt that the process of secularization is irreversible in them all?

There are of course many in Lutheran, Roman Catholic, and other churches who view secularization negatively. They look with nostalgia upon days gone by when the church was part of the very fabric of social life and traces of religion could be seen everywhere. The present inexorable shift toward secular autonomy is for them a sign that the kingdom of God has fallen upon hard times. This outlook in both Roman Catholic and Lutheran circles is quick to catalogue a *Syllabus of Errors* in the trend toward secularization. It is the encroachment of modern apostasy, they feel, and the church's task is to hold the line of Christian society in the face of increasing pressures from modern godlessness. Particularly among Roman Catholics, who are accustomed in many countries to exercise dominant political, legislative, and moral influence, many continue to fight a fierce rear guard action to preserve the church's weight in such matters. Accepting such thinking as Vatican II's *Decree on Religious Liberty*, for example, was a bitter pill for those of this outlook to swallow.

The negative reaction to secularization on the Lutheran side usually takes the form not of such attempts at repristination but rather resignation and capitulation. Having been pushed out of the secular world, the church contents itself with being custodian of the "religious" realm. Against the tendency of the church to deal with social problems, persons of this view express their anxiety that the church is selling out to secular currents and becoming just another secular social agency. This is of course an eminently legitimate concern, but it is often carried to such hypersensitive lengths that the church abdicates virtually any prophetic or active role in the secular realm.

On the whole, however, Roman Catholic and Lutheran theologians acknowledge secularization for what it is — a historical fact (with substantial biblical justification) which presents both difficulties and opportunities for the church and which calls for careful theological evaluation. They affirm in Gogarten's phrase, the legitimate "worldliness of the world."

Yet one must hasten to add that this acknowledgement has not narrowed their theological concern. Secularization has actually had an ironically paradoxical effect upon theology. The church's influence may be waning, but the scope of theology has broadened. In a certain sense the process of secularization has liberated theology. What we are witnessing in contemporary theology is not an expanding secular autonomy over against a shrinking sacred realm, but more accurately a growing theological comprehension of the whole world, which is not straitjacketed by an *a priori* sacred-secular dichotomy. Theology has cut the umbilical cord tying it exclusively to the "sacred half" of the world and has turned its full attention to all creation, unconscious of any sacred-secular fence dissecting it.

The fundamental reason for this broadened theological vision is this: Instead of seeing God working in the world primarily or only through the church, we have recaptured the biblical view of God's ceaseless activity in the world as sovereign creator of all things.[4] When the work of God is seen in this totality, a strict distinction between sacred and secular dissolves as irrelevant.

This wider scope of God's work is, of course, not a new discovery. Both Roman Catholics and Lutherans find the source of this outlook not only in the Scriptures but deeply imbedded in their own traditions as well. Both have always affirmed that God created and continues to preserve the world, but through the years both traditions permitted the relationship between the church and the world to drift into viewpoints which have now revealed their bankruptcy in the face of secularization.

Roman Catholicism upset this relationship first by a preoccupation with a sacramental system of God's work, where God's grace was transmitted virtually exclusively through the church's sacramental dispensation; and secondly, by papal claims to ecclesiastical sovereignty over secular affairs, symbolized most graphically by the shivering Emperor Henry IV appearing barefoot beneath the pope's window at Canossa; and then finally by Boniface VIII's calamitous 1302 bull *Unam Sanctam*. The first factor removed God's grace from creation and funnelled it through the "sacred" orders of the church. The second factor crystallized thinking into a sacred-secular mentality by setting the two against each other in terms of political jurisdiction.

Luther rejected ecclesiastical dominance over secular and political affairs by affirming that God ruled in both the worldly and the churchly realms. He reigned in the world through the orders of law and justice, and in the church through mercy and the gospel. This could have led to a fruitful and more expansive consideration of God's sovereignty and presence in the secular realm, but the turn which was in fact taken in succeeding generations of Lutheran theology stressed the distinction of these two realms, regiments or kingdoms of God's rule so drastically that the church had practically nothing to say or do in the worldly realm (although the state never did reciprocally take its finger wholly out of the church's pie in many Lutheran countries). Lutheranism also reinforced, though not intentionally, a view of the world as basically sinful by designating it as the locus for God's action through his "left hand," as it were, reserving for the church the gracious work of his "right hand."

At present both traditions are reassessing these patterns of thought. To say that we have realized anew the hand and activity of God in the secular world will of course strike nobody as an original or surprising observation, and most readers will wonder, "Is it really necessary to go over this again?" But this fact must be stated, because the impact of this realization has only begun to soak into our theological thinking, and it is safe to say that the far-reaching implications have only started to dawn upon the church and its ecumenical outlook.

If the world were by nature a worthless, fallen vale of wickedness, and *if* God revealed his grace and imparted his Spirit exclusively through the ecclesiastical sacraments, and *if* the church were the group of redeemed whose task it was solely to convert worldly sinners into its circumference, then our old ways of thinking would still be appropriate — and like it or not, these are the presuppositions behind much of the church's traditional mentality. If, however, we acknowledge that God is "in the world," then the relationship between church and world is altered radically and fundamentally from our usual pattern of thinking that only the church "brings God, Christ, and the Spirit" into the secular orders. If God is already present not only as the law-giving preserver of the social order (in the sense of the Lutheran *usus politicus legis*) but is also working redemptively and graciously among men, then we shall have to do some serious reexamination.

History presents us with a baffling mixture of the divine and the demonic, and the church must develop prophetic insight to identify these elements. We can no longer consider the secular world simply as the godless fallen order, but must look to discern the hand of God in the flow of history and human events outside the church. In what ways is God present in human history? How do we recognize him? How can the church "follow him" in his work? The church will even have to swallow hard and look for the signs of the triune God active in hostile ideologies and non-Christian religions. And yet in the midst of realizing God's all-encompassing presence, Christian theology must clearly and carefully assert both God's definitive and explicit revelation in Jesus Christ as well as his special presence in Word and sacrament. To affirm and explain the juxtaposition of God's ubiquitous presence in the world and his revealed presence in Word and Sacrament is one of the fundamentally urgent tasks of theology today.

The reliable boundaries between secular and sacred, sinful and sanctified have melted irrevocably away. The advent of secularization has dislodged the church from its accustomed place of respect in society; the theological vision which sees beyond a sacred-secular polarity to God's presence and action in all creation cuts away the foundations of one whose view of the church is merely "to bring God to a sinful world." In short, in this theological context all of us — Roman Catholics and Lutherans together with the whole church — find ourselves forced to ask, as does the title of a recent book by a Roman Catholic, "Do we need the church?" [5] The impact of secularization upon the church can not be overstated. This unfamiliar atmosphere of the modern world has produced in the church a period of intense and often hotly contested reexamination of its very existence. It is causing us to rethink from the bottom up the most basic questions of the church's being.

> . . . how is the church to interpret its existence in the world? This is the ecclesiological question which the historical phenomenon of secularization has forced upon the church.[6]

Secularization has not only pushed the question of the church's very existence into center stage, but has also altered our approach to the question. In thinking about the church, both Roman Catholics and Lutherans have traditionally set out by asking, "What is it?" The presupposition was that once we got our definition right in terms of the church *qua* church, then we could go on to deal with the church's relation to and mission in the "outside" world.

The Reformation itself hardened this approach. Having been excommunicated from Rome, the reformers bore the burden of proof that the Reformation church was indeed the true church and not schismatic or sectarian. As each side geared up to justify itself against the other, the whole question of the church turned introspective, each side proving that it represented the church in its true nature, structure, doctrine, and so on. The battle over the church revolved around the question of the true *notae ecclesiae,* and it raged with increasing intensity into the next generation in the monumental disputes between such men as Martin Chemnitz, Robert Bellarmine, Johann Gerhard, and their successors into the following generations. Any dogmatic concern with the outside world had to yield right of way to the settling of this more pressing polemic.

The circumstances of that day may have made this approach inevitable, but the situation of our day makes this point of departure seem strangely out of place. For now the challenge of the secular poses the problem from this side: "*Why* does the church exist in the world? What is it for?" Questions regarding the church's nature, true marks, structure, and authority, are important issues of course, but not antecedent to the prior and essential question of the church's purpose or mission. If the secular realm is conceded an autonomy and independence from churchly supervision, how does the church then relate to the secular at all? If God is active in the secular world, how can the church's mission align itself with God's own mission? These are the "if's" determining our ecclesiastical thinking today.

In short, whereas for centuries we have been accustomed to defining first the church's nature and then its mission, secularization has reversed these priorities. First the church must clarify its mission in the world, indeed, perhaps justify its existence in the world. Lutheran theologian Keith Bridston applies a principle of cybernetics in arguing that the church "must be described by verbs rather than nouns." [7] The articulation of the church's mission and purpose will imply a certain nature. Related questions of structure, ministry, and authority will then follow from these considerations. But first the church must define itself, and this definition must be made in reference to the whole world.

Though it is appropriate to speak about such a "reversal of priorities" brought about by secularization, one should warn lest this "reversal" become a swing of the pendulum to the other extreme. It would be more accurate to stress how interdependent the church's nature and mission are to one another. Any polarity between nature and mission is nonsense both from a biblical as well as a theological point of view. Neither is derived simply from the exigencies of the secular world, for both are given by God, and the scope of the church's existence transcends the world. Yet the church's nature and mission bestowed by God upon his church can never be separated from God's own activity in the secular world.

Contemporary reflection on the church in the world has been stimulated lately by the juxtaposition of two slogans, "God-church-world" and "God-world-church," made prominent by a provocative World Council of Churches Evangelism Report of western European scholars.[8] Though over-simplified, the contrast of these two formulas does echo this profound shift in today's thinking. In October, 1966, the Commission on Stewardship and Evangelism of the Lutheran World Federation held a consultation in Finland on the theme "The Structure of the Congregation in Mission" which dealt precisely with these questions. Bishop Werner Krusche of Leipzig set the problem in its theological context by referring to the WCC report and added:

> The order God-world-church corresponds to the facts: the fact that God relates primarily to the world, that the world is the center of his action, is seen even in the placement of the history of the "world" (Gen. 1-11) before the history of the covenant, but especially in its cardinal placement in John 3:16.[9]

The deliberations of this group were submitted for study at the 1970 LWF assembly in Evian-les-Bains, France, so that these problems will hopefully occupy the attention of a larger circle than just an inner *avant-garde* of theologians.

If we were to schematize traditional Lutheran thinking on this theme, we could picture a triangle with God on the top, one of the sides leading to the church, the other to the world. This is the standard Lutheran image, the two realms of God's work. What contemporary Lutheran scholars are now attempting to do is to complete the triangle by defining the nature of its third side, the horizontal line from the church to the world. When the triangle is completed, we see lines running both from God and from the church toward the world.

On the Lutheran side Friedrich Gogarten stands as a pre-war forerunner of this trend of thinking, and he laid down the guide-lines for much current thought with his careful distinction between a legitimate "secularization" and a self-sufficient, even idolatrous "secularism." By literally paying for his commitment to the secular world with his own life, Dietrich Bonhoeffer became almost the prototype of a theologian of secularization, and the corpus of his uncompleted thought has inspired countless followers to continue the unfolding of his ideas.

In reexamining the relationship of God, world, and the church today in theological terms, however, Roman Catholic theologians have pioneered far ahead of Lutherans. This may be because Roman Catholicism has traditionally treated the natural world as a more homogeneous element in its theological schema, whereas Lutheran theology has never worked itself wholly free from the taint of Flacius' radical pessimism, looking upon man every Sunday in the liturgy as "by nature sinful and unclean." The term "natural theology" strikes a pejorative ring in Lutheran ears, but a Roman Catholic finds solid precedence in Scholastic theology for incorporating "nature" into his theological scope.[10] Among Roman Catholic scholars one thinks immediately of the persuasive stimuli for renewed thinking provided by thinkers as Karl Rahner and Edward Schillebeeckx with their use of such concepts as "anonymous" and "implicit" Christianity.[11] Or we can cite the enormous influence exercised posthumously by Teilhard de Chardin, who envisioned far ahead of his time that everything in the universe representing man's secular striving is ultimately sacred. One might be skeptical of his vibrant optimism, but his thought has stirred a new appreciation for the secular in a whole new generation of theologians. Each of these men, plus many others, were and are attempting to define the reality of God present and working in the world *extra muros ecclesiae*, apart from the institutional church. They affirm God's gracious presence and work in the world and challenge the church to attune its own work to God's action. It is a bold and fruitful line of exploration which cannot help but have vast implications for the church's life and mission.

THE CHURCH IN THE SECULAR WORLD

If secularization has made the question of the church's existence doubly urgent, how are Roman Catholic and Lutheran thinkers reacting? What concept of mission is being formed in this new framework of inquiry?

Without taking space for an exhaustive survey of current ecclesiological thinking, it can be accurately said that the image which has emerged as the most appropriate description of the church's mission today is the church as *servant in and to the world*. The idea of a servant church is in part a reaction against the proud triumphalism on one hand and a religious isolationism on the other, both of which have plagued the church for a long time. But it is more than a reaction; it is a restoration of what many believe to be the church's true mode of existence in the world.

The understanding of the church's mission as service finds its source in a renewed Christological interest. If the church is to find its way in the world, the obvious point of reference would be to inquire about the life which its Lord lived in the world. This Christological inquiry focuses upon Christ's own relationship with the world. For several years in the past decade this concern has been reflected in various theological studies of the Lutheran World Federation around the general theme "The Quest for True Humanity and the Lordship of Christ." The new point of orientation was underscored by Ivar Asheim, former director of the LWF Department of Theology:

The important thing here is that in the concept of the lordship of Christ the point of emphasis has been shifted from the church to the world.[12]

Our Christological thinking must now relate to the Christian's role in the world; precisely in what way is Jesus Christ the Lord and Redeemer of this world?

In following this line of inquiry, the first half of the LWF study theme has claimed major attention: the quest for true humanity. Secular man longs for "true humanity," for abundant life. A Christian is one who believes that he has not only found the example of true humanity in his Lord, but who believes that this Lord offers the same fullness of life to men. The Vatican Council expressed this belief:

> For God's Word . . . entered the world's history as a perfect man . . . He animates, purifies, and strengthens those noble longings too by which the human family strives to make its life more human and to render the whole earth submissive to this goal.[13]

Since this is a universal striving, this aspect of the gospel is pointedly relevant to the secular world, and both Roman Catholic and Lutheran theologians are therefore inquiring anew into this theme, the humanity of Christ.

What is the nature of this true humanity which Christ personifies and offers to man today? From the books of the New Testament, Jesus stands out as a man who lived in full harmony with God and man. His unity with his Father was complete; his sense of brotherhood and solidarity with man knew no bounds of social class or religious affiliation. He healed Jews, Samaritans, a Roman slave, a Canaanite girl, and the Syrophoenician woman's daughter. He lived by the spirit of the law, never permitting institutional inhibitions or legal technicalities to stand in his way. Jesus of Nazareth was, in short, himself a *servant*. ". . . even as the Son of man came not to be served but to serve, and to give his life as a ransom for many" (Matt. 20:28).

His servanthood was directed toward the whole man, toward the fullness of humanity. Whatever condition left an individual less than whole he healed, whether a crippled limb, blind eyes, deaf ears, hungry stomachs, the moral degradation of Mary Magdalene, the dishonest greed of Zacchaeus, the self-righteousness of some Pharisees, the busyness of Martha, or the timidity of his own disciples. To all of them he offered the hope of a full life on earth as well as an eternal life with God.

On the Lutheran side it was Dietrich Bonhoeffer more than anybody else who signalled this Christological orientation around the servanthood of Christ. His characterization of Christ as "a man for others" has become a theological household word in the whole church, especially after J. A. T. Robinson's best-selling *Honest to God.* This phrase has then spilled over into ecclesiological thinking, as one finds for example in the title of the evangelism study of the World Council of Churches: *The Church for Others.* As Jesus was a servant to men, so also does the church follow its Lord as servant.

There is of course nothing in this notion which is limited to Protestants. The renaissance of the understanding of the church as servant in the world is a realization of all Christians that this is indeed the true calling of the church in this secular age. The second session of the Vatican Council was to begin its deliberations on *The Church,* and the newly elected Pope Paul VI opened the session with these words:

> Let the world know this: The church looks at the world with profound understanding, with sincere admiration and with the sincere intention not of conquering it, but of serving it. . . .[14]

Fr. John B. Sheerin commented, "I feel sure that the Protestant observers said a fervent 'Amen' to this concept of the church as servant." [15] He was right.

The church's ministry as servant must then be directed toward secular man, the whole man, not just a part of him, such as his soul, or religious side. In the opening paragraphs of the Council document addressing all mankind we read of the church's intention in the modern world:

> Hence the pivotal point of our total presentation will be man himself, whole and entire, body and soul, heart and conscience, mind and will.[16]

This *Pastoral Constitution on the Church in the Modern World* is one of the remarkable achievements of Vatican II, not only for its distinction of being the only document originating rather impulsively from the Council floor, but because it reflects the shift of the church's concentration on its own problems to attention to the problems of the world around it. Theo Westow, an English Roman Catholic, describes how this document set out to "bring the church down to earth ... to open new vistas" by making clear that *"the church is wholly involved in the human condition* and cannot live ... in self-centered superior isolation." [17]

Jesus' life of service becomes, therefore, the blueprint for the church's service, and the church seeks to define its mission from the New Testament accounts of Jesus' life. In a statement later adopted by the Board of Social Ministry of the Lutheran Church in America, William Lazareth writes:

> Hence, all authentic Christian service — whether performed individually or corporatively — must faithfully and lovingly conform to the distinctive style of life revealed by Jesus Christ ... Christians are called in the obedience of faith to minister in and for the world as the servant church of the Servant Lord.[18]

Jesus' concern for the poor and outcast, his solicitude for the bodily sick, his warnings against the worldly wealth which eats at the soul, his ability to transform people through his life, and so on — all these become marks of the church's service in the secular world. This service conveys the gospel at its fullest, a concern for the whole man.

Two words have become popular to describe this ministry of service. The first is "humanization." In this technological world man finds himself a mere unit of production, a faceless worker on an assembly line or in a corporate structure, and his biography is recorded in the punched holes of an IBM punch card. As if the words were written specifically for our century, the Christian finds in the New Testament the promises of a fully human life and offers them to modern man trapped in a sterile existence. "I have come that they may have life, and have it abundantly" (John 10:10). This is surely a moment in history ripe for the church's message of "humanization" in the richest sense of the word!

The second word is the ancient Jewish benediction *shalom*. In his book *Reconciliation: The Function of the Church*, for example, Roman Catholic scholar Eugene C. Bianchi outlines his hopes for a "church of shalom" by recovering the depth and breadth of this word:

> The whole unfolding of biblical history represents the Lord's struggle to establish the reconciling peace, the shalom, among men and with himself. The Hebrew word "shalom" . . . derives from a root which at once signifies wholeness, harmony, integrity. Thus shalom describes the state of men who live on earth in reconciliation with nature, themselves, their neighbors, and God.[19]

In a modern world torn by hostility, this word, whose origins date from the dawn of history, expresses superbly what the gospel of Christ brings to man.

It is immediately clear that this kind of Christology ministers directly to the needs and aspirations of today's secular man. The problems of the modern world — automated assembly lines, huge corporations, people packed into urban centers, the widening gap between rich and poor — all cry out for a pattern of truly fulfilled human living. It is no wonder that contemporary theology has turned to this aspect of Christology, the perfect humanity of Christ. Its message is that of Pontius Pilate before the Jerusalem masses: *Ecce homo.* Behold the man, the one true man who has come to make us all men. One of the reasons for Martin Luther King's charismatic ministry was reflected in a sign carried by demonstrators in the Memphis, Tennessee, confrontations, "I AM A MAN." Rev. King was convinced that the Christian gospel carried within itself the resources for restoring manhood and dignity to the poor and oppressed.

This Christological emphasis in no way intends to diminish Jesus' divinity. It senses that dialog with the modern world can be most fruitfully inaugurated at the level of Christ's common humanity with men, and that this facet of Christology has been woefully neglected until now. Yet here again theology faces the familiar pitfall of the swinging pendulum: there is a danger of reducing Christology to that which seems suitable to us now and of emphasizing one image of Christ's work to the exclusion of all others. For example, if "Jesus as servant and example toward full humanity" were the sum and substance of Christology, such central concepts as grace and forgiveness would hardly remain integral elements of our outlook. If Christology focuses only upon an *imitatio Christi,* an imitation of Christ's life, where does that put the cross? Or the resurrection for that matter? If all Christology is summarized in service, then will we not find ourselves justifying our Christian existence not by God's mercy or grace, but by the quality of our service, that is, a justification by our works? Finally, Jesus of Nazareth was doubtlessly concerned about physical sickness, hunger, and other worldly things, but in the last analysis did he not measure the destiny of man in terms of his relationship with God; the New Testament kingdom of God was not a reorganized social order but a new humanity. Jesus was playing for higher stakes than for comfortable worldly living; he came first of all to restore man's eternal life with God. Any ministry of service which settles for less is a reduction of Jesus' own ministry.

It is all too tempting to present to the secular world a Christology which the world finds desirable, palatable, and attractive. The servanthood of Christ is indeed an aspect of his work uniquely suited to the gospel proclamation of our day. It does not replace the Christology handed down in our traditions but rather complements and enriches our total Christological and ecclesiastical views.

The church's new attitude to the secular world and its outreach in service presents a host of other theological problems. How can we steer the Scylla of secular optimism, which sees divine action in every movement urging change and opposing the status quo, and the Charybdis of secular pessimism, for which the hand of God in the world is totally undetectible and incognito? How does one reconcile a *theologia crucis,* a theology of worldly suffering and defeat, or the biblical "suffering servant," with the militancy and crusading triumphalism often seen among radical Christian activists, yet without lapsing into the equally false extreme of resigned pietistic quietism? While applauding the church's growing concern for all mankind, Bishop Lesslie Newbigin warns against a "false eschatology which finds its ultimate meaning in the development of the human community," because such a concept of a servant church would lose the full dimensions of the biblical Servant of the Lord.[20] According to this view,

> everything is subordinated to the demand that the Church should be relevant to the needs of the world. The Church then becomes a rather ineffective auxiliary to a variety of social and political movements, and loses its authentic character as the bearer of a Gospel which can deal with sin, guilt and death (p. 119).

Then there is also the perennial question: how can we discern God's presence in the secular world with any degree of certainty? Christian activists are quick to spot signs of God's hand in practically every area of social change. Others see only demonic chaos, where one demon is eliminated only to be succeeded by seven others, each worse than the first. The theological implications of the church's engagement in the secular world will demand careful study of these and many other problems in the years to come.

It is obvious that this whole line of thinking indicates a thorough restudy of what we understand by Christian missions. In many ways it runs headlong into the main stream of traditional missionary thinking, and an intense rethinking of missionary activity is in fact going on in both Roman Catholic and Protestant churches. For those to whom missions means "bringing God into a godless world and pagans into the church's membership rolls," this openness to secularity will appear dangerously corrosive of our mission enterprise.

Current thinking sees the task of missions as much broader than the *plantatio ecclesiae,* although this is not to be given up. But the church's role in a "nonchristian country" (as if the church were not a diaspora minority in every country) is now more concerned with its activity as a serving church than with its numerical "conversion rate." This may be the shape of the church's missionary role in the future out of sheer necessity, since many countries who resent outright proselytizing still welcome health, educational, and technological help from Christian missions. In the context of this broader outlook, this latter work is fully as "Christian" and appropriate to Christian missions as overt conversions. Again, Roman Catholic thinking has spearheaded new approaches to the question of missions.

One such example of renewed missionary thinking is *The Wider Ecumenism* by a Roman Catholic missionary in Tanzania, Fr. Eugene Hillman, C.S.Sp.[21] Fr. Hillman subtitles his study "Anonymous Christianity and the Church" and proposes in his preface to continue what he calls the theme of what might have been Bonhoeffer's next book had he lived: "The Church is her true self only when she exists for humanity" (p. 13 f.). In the first sections of the book he shows how the church has worked itself into an impossible impasse by thinking that it has a monopoly on God's grace. Christ came for all men, and the work of God's grace can be seen everywhere. The second part of the book deals with the question: if God's grace works among peoples everywhere, why then the Christian church at all? His answer provides a firm basis and program for Christian mission in a secular world.

> The new people of God are saints and sinners who are called out of every tribe and tongue and people and nation. Their explicit union of faith and hope and charity is a living testimony of that reconciliation which brings order out of chaos, good out of evil, acceptance out of revolt, truth out of contradiction, and unity out of estrangement. The church is thus an effective sign of the universal brotherhood of men. . . . The salutary significance of the community of explicit Christian faith is rooted in the Incarnation from which the Church, as the sacramentally symbolic continuation of this mystery in the extension of different historical times and places, derives her reason for existence, her meaning and necessity for humanity as a whole (pp. 85 f., 87 f.).

Proclaiming and following Christ in mission is the heart of the church's existence because it believes that in Jesus Christ God was incarnate in human history, working for the redemption of all men. Grace is everywhere present, but the church points to the fullness of this grace in Christ. The church's very "presence in the world," to repeat a term often used especially by Roman Catholic thinkers, as an explicit testimony to this grace is a mark of its mission.

Seeing God's grace in the secular world not only involves this expanded vision of the church's mission into all areas of human need, but also implies a more positive attitude toward other religions as well. The term "wider ecumenism" means for Roman Catholic scholar S. T. Balasuriya that "ecumenism in this wider sense is the effort to understand the religious convictions of others and to search for what their religion is or could be in the divine plan for history."[22] Vatican II's *Declaration on the Relationship of the Church to Non-Christian Religions* also reveals an openness to appreciate the positive elements of other religions.

> The Catholic Church rejects nothing which is true and holy in these religions. She looks with sincere respect upon those ways of conduct and of life, those rules and teachings which, though differing in many particulars from what she holds and sets forth, nevertheless often reflect a ray of that Truth which enlightens all men.[23]

This note is echoed in the *Decree on Missions* (9, 11), although on the whole that document outlines the role of missions in a more traditional fashion than the more venturesome *Declaration on Non-Christian Religions*. This fact only illustrates that this kind of thinking is still in the exploratory stage and has not yet been fully resolved or harmonized with the usual formulations, neither in Roman Catholicism nor in Lutheranism. It is noteworthy that in both traditions the study of evangelism and missions, once a moribund theological backwater in the curriculum, has now been propelled to the center of theological thinking. This accentuates the fact that the relationship of the church to the secular, Christian, and non-Christian world has not only claimed the spotlight of theological attention, but has indeed turned much traditional thinking topsy-turvy.

Yet this openness to the secular world and the affirmation of God's pervading presence is not "syncretistic" in the usual sense of the word. Such an outlook is not one which combines elements of various religions into a big stew. It is consciously and uncompromisingly Christian, because it believes that in Jesus Christ God was fully present and revealed, and that Jesus represents a fully human being as God had intended man to be. God is present and active in secular affairs, and the Christian is in the unique position of being able to measure and recognize his "anonymous" activity against the explicit pattern of Jesus' life. There is no inner contradiction in seeing traces of God in other religions while believing in the uniqueness of Christianity.

These first two sections have outlined the theological backdrop of secular ecumenism, specifically the repercussions of secularization upon our thinking. With these developments, secular ecumenism was virtually inevitable. To this impact on ecumenism we now turn.

SECULAR ECUMENISM AND UNITY

It is the presupposition of secular ecumenism that these urgent problems of secularization and the modern world are the most important issues of the church's existence today. A "secular ecumenist" sets out from the conviction that contemporary ecumenical thinking and practice should be formed more by these issues than by yesterday's polemics. Therefore, it follows that his sense of unity is determined primarily by the unity which he finds among those of all churches concerning these problems.

Many speak of secular ecumenism as a new dimension of unity, another level added to the ecumenism of bilateral-multilateral church relations, the ecumenism of national and international agencies, and the ecumenism among local congregations. This is true, but the inherent nature of secular ecumenism imposes a new perspective on all the other types of ecumenism.

In the last analysis — and this is the important fact for us to realize here — secular ecumenism is a new concept of unity altogether, a concept which not only confronts the churches with a new view of unity but which is based upon the church's very mission in the world.

Individual churches have traditionally measured unity in terms of what each considers the essential elements of the church. The mark of the true church for Roman Catholicism, for example, is its unbroken continuity of faith and tradition, preserved and symbolized by the episcopal college of bishops with the bishop of Rome at its head. Rome measures the unity of the church, therefore, in terms of belonging to this continuous historical tradition. The first generation of Wittenberg reformers believed that the most essential mark of the true church was the unobscured gospel of God's grace, given to the church through the means of Word and Sacrament. From this standpoint the preservation of a hierarchical continuity was not essential in the same way as the preservation of the true

biblical gospel and its work in church life. The reformers, therefore, measured unity on the basis of what they considered the
heart of the church's existence, namely the gift of God's grace in
Word and Sacrament.

For the true unity of the church it is enough to agree concerning
the teaching of the Gospel and the administration of the sacraments.[24]

John Calvin and the Swiss reformers went a step further by
replacing the episcopalian system of church structure with the
rule of elders, which they believed to be in closer harmony with
Scripture, and which in turn became for the Reformed an essential
mark of the church. The historical circumstances of the formation
of the Anglican church were such that Anglicans have regarded
their episcopal succession from the apostles together with their
communion with the archbishop of Canterbury as the distinctive
mark of their churchly existence and hence a measure of unity
with the Anglican Communion.

So it has gone — each church measuring unity by that which it
considers the essential mark and nature of its being. Into this
context comes secular ecumenism. In one sense its criterion of unity
does conform to this traditional pattern: it too measures unity on
what it considers to be fundamental to the essence of the church.

And what does secular ecumenism consider fundamentally
essential to the church's being? — this theological conviction of
God's presence in the secular world and a commitment to the
church's role as servant to the whole secular man, that is, a theological consensus around those issues which we have presented in
the preceding two sections. It is a unity of those who believe that
the church exists primarily to serve the secular world.

Secular ecumenism has jolted the normal flow of the ecumenical
movement because its banner of unity cuts clean through denominational boundary lines. For a secular ecumenist the traditional
ecclesiastical borders signify very little. A common outlook and
commitment toward the existence and mission of the Christian
church today is a more basic measure of true unity for him than
the perseverance of the church boundaries inherited from centuries
past. It has often been lamented that the student generation of
today lacks a sense of history. This is true, but this fact does have

its laudable as well as lamentable aspects. At any rate, today's theological students are notoriously unconcerned about many traditional ecumenical questions and determine their lines of fellowship far more according to contemporary issues.

> A new type of ecumenism is meanwhile emerging which was hardly anticipated by professional ecumenists who preoccupied themselves with cooperation and reunion in church institutional terms ... other Christians from a great assortment of backgrounds are meeting each other in the secular sphere, in civil rights demonstrations, in peace movements, in professional societies, in a common search for viable approaches to urban problems, in the fields of education, housing, jobs, and in trying to minister to those who are hooked on dope or drugs. The seminary student today is more ecumenical than his professors, for while his professors are carefully weighing the doctrinal proprieties of how far they dare go, the student gleefully goes all the way, and actually scorns this "toe in the water" type of ecumenical attitude ... Denominationalism is overcome not by theologians sitting in their studies or at conference tables, but it is being undercut, whether we like it or not, by those who are actually carrying on their ministries in the secular world.[25]

One wonders what will be the long-term effect upon ecumenism when these young people mature and take their places in church leadership. What will their attitude be then as mature churchmen in responsible positions toward the doctrinal and institutional levels of ecumenism which they scorn as students? Will there be a backlash, a resurgence of interest for traditional ecumenical problems of doctrine? It seems hardly likely, but perhaps some of their enthusiasm will be sobered by realizing that these knotty doctrinal issues which have divided us for centuries cannot be simply swept under the rug or waved away. They may not seem as important as the spirit of polemics once made them to be, but they still remain with us. It is a fascinating topic for speculation to envisage what will happen when the mood of secular ecumenism will permeate throughout the church. How many previously divisive problems will fade from the scene for lack of contemporary relevance, and which problems will stay with us until met squarely and resolved? Secular ecumenism has not only captured the allegiance of vast

numbers of the younger generation, but it spills out infectiously
into other aspects of ecumenism. By working and serving together
in streets and slums as Christ's servants, people discover that the
ecclesiastical barriers no longer loom so formidable as previously
thought. Secular ecumenism can therefore ease the way for the
ecumenism of doctrinal discussion by creating an atmosphere of
cooperation in mission. The council fathers of Vatican II sensed
this fact when they concluded the paragraph urging broad collaboration on secular problems among all Christians by saying,
"... through such cooperation all believers in Christ are able to
learn easily... how the road to the unity of Christians may be
made smooth." [26] Reflecting on this Decree on *Ecumenism* and its
effect on Roman Catholic ecumenism, Gregory Baum suggests that
the traditional order of ecumenical progress should be reversed.
Instead of first solving the inner-churchly problems of division and
then turning to the world,

> The Vatican Council acknowledges that through such an
> involvement [in secular society] the church herself will be
> changed, find new ways of being faithful to the Gospel, and
> be redeemed of many of the ills, including the divisions, which
> at present beset her life.[27]

Thus secular ecumenism not only presents a new kind of unity,
but also invigorates the traditional ecumenical endeavors.

One thing is certain. Though secular ecumenism is not primarily
interested in the usual forms of ecumenism between church bodies,
it gives this level of ecumenism a powerful stimulus. If the church
is to be a living and dynamic symbol of the gospel of reconciliation
in Christ to all men, any bitterness and lack of brotherhood among
Christian churches is a disheartening sign that even among those
who share the fullness of the gospel there is a lack of the very
fellowship which they proclaim. Ill-feeling among Christians both
impedes and discredits the gospel. Secular ecumenism provides all
forms of ecumenism with added urgency.

Yet secular ecumenism is by no means a cure-all panacea on the
ecumenical scene. Its appearance points out the ironic shift in
ecumenism: secular ecumenism exerts a force for a unity of service
whose magnetic field draws from all denominations, yet it simul-

taneously exposes divisions *within* churches which threaten to be more disruptive and painful than the divisions *between* churches. With those who share his vision of the church as servant in the secular world, regardless to which church they belong, a secular ecumenist feels a deep sense of unity around that which he considers essential. But with those who criticize his involvement he feels a sharp and discouraging estrangement, even if such critics are fellow members of his own church.

An example of secular ecumenism was the series of massive demonstrations at Selma, Alabama, in 1965. Here priests, nuns, pastors, and lay-people from all churches both black and white converged and marched arm in arm in a conscientiously Christian witness, along with Jews and other non-Christians. Their actions brought them together as Christians and simultaneously forged a common humanitarian bond with all men who shared the same sense of outrage against injustice and prejudice. At that moment they were one with other Christians and with other humanitarians in a kind of unity whose depth surprised even themselves.

Yet every one who marched in Selma went home to pointed criticism from members of his own church for such a demonstration. Here they sensed a disunity with their fellow churchmen which cut at the very center of what they thought was a fundamental summons to Christian witness and mission. Our traditional concept of unity — belonging to the same institution in agreement with the same confessions of past centuries — seemed altogether superficial in this context!

It is becoming increasingly obvious that the divisions within churches are more real than the divisions between them. Certainly they are more acrimoniously disputed. Relations between churches are steadily improving both in congeniality and understanding, while at the same time relations within any given church are steadily polarizing into fronts where congeniality is vanishing and fraternity has given way to distrust. In every church "conservatives" and "liberals" — the labels never fit, but the reader will recognize what is intended — are digging in against each other. And the battle lines are formed on precisely the issues of secular ecumenism, that is, the extent and the means of the church's involvement in the secular world.

This phenomenon produces some odd configurations. An English Roman Catholic writer noted that many Roman Catholics feel closer to the Anglican professor E. L. Mascall than to their own Hans Küng, and that Prof. Mascall is religiously nearer the Roman Catholic Archbishop of Westminster, Cardinal John Heenan, than he is to his fellow Anglican, J. A. T. Robinson, former bishop and now chaplain of Christ's College in Cambridge.[28] In the United States an ultraconservative Lutheran newssheet vilifies even relatively conservative Lutherans as liberal while expressing sympathy with the Catholic Traditionalist Movement of Fr. Gommar DePauw. In countless communities one can find priests or pastors who are frustrated by a disparity of views with their own colleagues but who build deep friendships with clergymen from other sides of the denominational fence who share their views regarding church mission.[29]

Feelings on this score run deep and cannot help but exercise a profound effect on ecumenism. A Protestant pastor writing in a Roman Catholic magazine warns, "As Christians finally draw together across denominational lines, they are being threatened by a major new division cutting across all others...."[30] Secular ecumenism is therefore paradoxically both a uniting force sweeping through all denominations and yet far more divisive than any other factor in today's churches. After busying themselves with reconciling the divisive confessional problems between churches through painstaking theological work, ecumenists now discover their own individual churches being torn apart over contemporary issues.

What have we gained in solving the warmed-over problems of past centuries if the really crucial problems of the present day produce new and deeper divisions? Does it not suggest that the more urgent need of ecumenism today is to confront these intrachurch divisions between right and left, conservative and liberal? Secular ecumenism may be a providential bridge forging ties between the church and the world, but if it abandons continual dialog, whether out of self-righteousness or impatience, with those other Christians who hesitate to accept its aims and programs, it will prove self-defeating to the very cause of unity it seeks to promote.

OIKUMENE: "THE WHOLE INHABITED WORLD"

The word *oikumene* has traveled a circuitous route. It began as "the whole inhabited world," but the Christian church baptized it as "the whole church," and it was later narrowed to "the whole of a single church." As the ecumenical movement has been steadily embracing a growing number of churches, the word has lately been regaining weight, and with secular ecumenism the path of *oikumene* comes around full circle to include once more "the whole inhabited world." Bishop Newbigin calls secular ecumenism as "a widespread sense among men of all races that the human family is one and that everything which in practice denies this is an offense against God," and observes that this conviction "has led many Christians to feel that the real task for our day is to manifest the unity of mankind rather than to manifest the unity of the church." [31]

Ultimately these theological trends which we have been discussing lead to this fact: the object of God's mission in this world is the whole secular world. The church is neither the exclusive object of God's work nor the end of his action, though it is all too easy to slip into the kind of thinking which sees the church as the place where God works those purposes which sin has made unattainable in the secular world. The church is more precisely the instrument of God's action in this world.

What God wants for men he wants for all men. He desires reconciliation and healing for the wounds of mankind. Wherever there is hostility among men, groups hating or battling each other, persons suffering oppression and exploitation from unjust social structures, people whose lack of education dooms them to little better than an animal level of existence — these are the places where the message of Christianity must be directed, for there is also the mission of God in the world.

It goes almost without saying, therefore, that where Christians share this sense of mission, they disregard the boundaries of denominationalism and cooperate with one another instinctively. Vatican II envisaged such service derived from Christ's servanthood, noting that it has already become a force for unity and urging it to expand:

Cooperation among all Christians vividly expresses that bond which already unites them, and it sets in clearer relief the features of Christ the Servant. Such cooperation, which has already begun in many countries, should be ever increasingly developed, particularly in regions where a social and techno-logical evolution is taking place. . . . Christians should also work together in the use of every possible means to relieve the afflictions of our times, such as famine and natural dis-aster, illiteracy and poverty, lack of housing, and the unequal distribution of wealth.[32]

Among those who see the church's mission as service, this social ecumenism is taken quite for granted as a necessary part of the church's work. Such a person takes it for granted because it is not the end of ecumenism. For him ecumenism transcends the inner-churchly relations of social cooperation, doctrinal understanding or organizational merger. Since ecumenism encompasses for him the whole of mankind, he views inner-Christian ecumenism with almost a utilitarian interest. Churches united and/or cooperating in fellowship furnish a more creditable witness and a more effective resource for this wider unity in the world. Improved relations between churches are a necessary prerequisite for the real goal of ecumenism, that is, the very mission of the church as it strives toward unity and brotherhood in the world of men.[33]

The study document presented to the 1970 Lutheran World Federation assembly applied this wider perspective to the concept of unity. Beginning with the conviction that Jesus Christ "is still at work in the church, in order to bring peace and unity to man-kind," it follows that "the search for unity among churches is also subordinated to this goal and is aligned with the church's great commission of reconciling man with God and of men with one another." [34] The document provides in general a refreshing stimulus for Lutherans the world over to consider anew the intent of the Augsburg Confession's statement on unity (Article VII), particu-larly in terms of contemporary insights into the social factors, the nature and purpose of church confessions, the question of church fellowship and other matters. The study concludes with a view of unity which embraces all creation:

Ecumenical endeavor, which finds its life in the given unity,

and which at the same time reaches out to the promised unity,
will never seek church unity for its own sake, but will seek it
rather as a tool for the reconciliation of all men and as a
sign of the new creation, which God himself brings about in
judgment and in grace (p. 50).

Taking inner-Christian cooperation for granted, secular ecumenism considers the fact that it seeks to ally itself with all forces
and movements working toward these same humanitarian ends as
the genuinely ecumenical mark of its work. A secular ecumenist
demonstrating or lobbying for more equitable justice or fair housing, for example, welcomes collaboration from another Christian,
a Jewish rabbi, a Socialist, a Black Panther, or a Hindu. His immediate concern is not party labels but whether that person shares
these same goals and is willing to join efforts toward these ends.

In contrast to his view of inner-Christian ecumenism, he does not
consider this wider dimension of cooperation from a purely utilitarian standpoint. Working in and with the secular world is for
him the essence of ecumenism, for only through such broad action
can one align himself with the work of God in the world. Where
men are yearning and striving for such things as *shalom,* equality,
brotherhood, justice, and peace, there the secular ecumenist sees
the hand of God's Spirit. God's presence might be incognito,
"anonymous," or "implicit," but these signs are to him unmistakable
traces of the divine spark, God working in the muddy vicissitudes
of human history. Because God is not present clearly (as in the
incarnate Christ) or explicitly (as in the church's sacraments), the
secular ecumenist does not probe deeply for motives among his
secular fellow workers, but is resolutely convinced of Jesus' maxim,
"You will know them by their fruits" (Matt. 7:20), and that where
the fruits are good, the tree must ultimately have roots in the work
of God.

Very few would dispute in principle the church's social ministry
as servant in the secular world. Nor would many deny the principle
of allying with secular forces where possible toward worthwhile
ends, even though they may not be as confident of God's presence
in such forces as others. It is in practice where the dissensions and
controversies lie. It would not be inaccurate to say that the principle
of secular ecumenism has proved to be ecumenical, but the practice

unecumenical, that is, an increase in charitable and social concern is drawing churches together, but the manner and extent in which this ministry should be carried out has stoked the heat of many a controversy. Churches united on the commission to serve the secular world are divided on the practical means of their involvement.

It was much easier when Christians directed their charitable and social work toward suffering individuals, avoiding the problems of corporate society, and worked mainly with other Christians (usually even within their own church), mistrusting the forces and agencies of secular society. But a secular ecumenist commits himself to serve all men, challenging the evils of society as well as alleviating the burdens of individuals, and working with all like-minded people toward these goals. He, therefore, cannot help but find himself not only with strange bedfellows, nor can he avoid uneasy, ambiguous situations. He is continually vulnerable to attacks from moral purists who insist upon keeping their ethical hands and consciences clean through a policy of isolation.

There are many who seek to solve the problem by fencing the church's secular involvement off from certain areas. A large number of Christians would support the church building hospitals, adoption agencies, homes for unwed mothers, and children's homes, but draw the line at the church's "getting involved in politics," even when such political involvement might help eliminate the need for adoption agencies, homes for unwed mothers, and children's homes. Of course, there is a legitimate danger for a church to dabble in partisan politics, or to make moral judgments without knowing the salient facts. But for a church to approve a program giving slum children free breakfasts without battling the underlying reasons why slum homes are not providing or cannot provide the breakfasts is an evasion of the real issues. Nor is it consistent for a church itself to avoid political issues while urging its members to vigorous political involvement.

Even where the issues of right and wrong may be clear, the actual program a church should adopt is never so unambiguous. Even for a church or agency which is of one mind to help improve race relations, for example, it is extremely difficult for the church or any other agency to formulate a plan which will in all its aspects please even those it seeks to aid.

Anybody embroiled in the turmoil of social upheaval finds himself surrounded by mixed motives. There may be many, Christian and non-Christian, working toward the same ends, and the secular ecumenist soon discovers himself in the midst of a crossfire of clashing ulterior motives. In South America, for instance, everyone acknowledges that many countries are in the grip of a privileged oligarchy, where the rich minority (often including the church establishment) prosper midst the miserable poverty of the masses. A growing number of Christian clergy and lay people, especially the young, find this inconsistent with their faith and are unwilling to remain passive to the evil. They join the forces of change and therewith find themselves in a welter of thorny dilemmas. They may believe in non-violence, but they cannot escape association with those who are collecting weapons for a bloody confrontation. They act out of love for the masses, but they are allied with those who would not hesitate to throw a Molotov cocktail into a crowd of civilians. They would be demonstrating side-by-side with Communists who seek to manipulate the forces of reform to install their own oppressive oligarchy. If they succeed to bring the establishment down, they may have plunged the country into more suffering than even before. And so it goes.

Even though large numbers of Christians might accept the principles of secular ecumenism, the fact will remain that as soon as one plants both feet in human history there are no unimpeachably pure solutions. The secular ecumenist might glimpse the hand of God in the forces of social change, but he cannot overlook the ever present demonic elements there too. Anybody who claims to speak with sweeping confidence and unquestioning certainty about the church's cooperation with secular movements is either superficial or naive. It is not that simple. How often churchmen are defiantly certain of options which stand in direct contrast to each other. Yet the church cannot afford to sit on the sidelines immobilized by a trembling uncertainty or by demands of moral perfection.

The church is faced with a complex array of ancient and new problems. War is as old as mankind, for example, but the bomb puts the matter in a new light. The church will need to muster the best brainpower at its disposal to deal with these issues in the next decades.

One of the difficulties is that secular ecumenism is new enough that it has not yet thought through many of these matters with sufficient clarity. Until now it has been fueled by rhetoric more notable for its exuberance and conviction than for adequate reflection on theological implications. It has been swift to act, often in reaction to the flabby apathy toward action among churches, sometimes without a sober appraisal of its goals. A superb example of praiseworthy but fuzzy aspiration is the very headline of secular ecumenism: "the unity of man." What on earth is that? The utopian vision of Isaiah, where nations mold their weapons into plows and where the wolf and lion leave the lamb and calf at peace unmolested? To what extent can such a picture of perfection be the goal of a church's program? How can the church reconcile its hope for bringing about a "unity of man" with the fact that the Gospel of Christ is a scandal and offense to man, which Jesus predicted would set even families against each other?

Lesslie Newbigin notes how the phrase "the unity of mankind" has today a powerful emotional appeal.[35] A Buddhist, Marxist, and Christian alike can speak about man's unity with deep feeling, yet between them there are sharply contradictory ideas on what constitutes this unity and on what means are needed to achieve this unity. Bishop Newbigin reminds the church that its vision of unity has always been that "in Jesus alone is the true unity of mankind to be found" (p. 130).

> The Bible gives us no ground for believing that God has other plans for the unity of mankind than that which he has set forth in Jesus Christ and of which he has made the church to be first fruit, sign and instrument. . . . The only program for the unity of mankind about which the church can speak with confidence is the one which was announced by him who said: "I, when I am lifted up from the earth, will draw all men to myself" (pp. 131 f.).

We shall need a great deal of exacting deliberation on what we mean with this extraordinarily popular phrase, "the unity of mankind." [36]

A more distressing aspect is to consider the probability of the church's fulfilling this high aspiration toward reconciliation and unity among men. It is one thing to *say* that the church should be an instrument for brotherhood and unity among all men; it is quite another thing to *be* it. As a potential force the church commands the massive resources of millions of believers in the world's richest countries and solidly established native churches in the under-developed areas, but what are the signs that this sleeping giant will awake?

The record thus far does not warrant unbounded optimism. What has the church done for peace in this century? The two great world wars were fought almost exclusively among the "Christian countries." Today the churches talk a lot about peace, but what have they done, and what can they do, to implement their talk? There were countless tales of heroic Christian charity work during the Nigerian-Biafran war, but how could the church as church have acted to put an end to such a conflict? Individual Christians are devoting their lives to service in the slums, but will the corporate churches plunge wholeheartedly into these problems? To consider what could be done if every Christian in a country would give just one day's wages to such causes is a staggering thought!

Yet it is too early to pass a verdict on the church's performance. The theological outlook formed by the church's existence in a secularized world is still in its adolescent years and has yet to grow to maturity in all levels of the church. It is a way of thinking which must still push its path through misunderstanding and resistance, and it must sharpen and clarify its own position. One can not yet say that the church will not rise to the challenge, despite the plentiful prophets of doom who have already thrown up their hands in despair.

Does not the question of the last two paragraphs bring us back to the theme of this volume's introduction, namely the renewal of the church? In terms of church history, it is only recently that the church has found itself surrounded by a secular world in which it has had to define its role. Secular ecumenism has grown suddenly into a major force in Christendom, and the convictions which motivate it are bound to spread among greater numbers of Christians in the future. Whether or not it will fulfill its commitment to serve is nothing other than the challenge to renewal.

NOTES

1. J. B. Sheerin, C.S.P., "American Christians and Secular Ecumenism," in *Unitas*, Summer, 1967, p. 104. See also E. A. Smith, *Journal of Ecumenical Studies*, Spring, 1968, p. 343: "Secular ecumenism is an awakening of Christians to the social bearing of their faith and united action on urgent problems."

2. For a lengthy list of examples of this sort of joint effort, see "Fruits of Cooperation," the concluding chapter in H. H. Ward's source book *Documents of Change* (Englewood Cliffs, N.J.: Prentice-Hall, 1966, pp. 410 f.).

3. Although it is virtually impossible to chart exactly the genealogy of the term secular ecumenism, we might date its birth from an address delivered in December, 1963, by M. M. Thomas in Mexico City to the WCC Commission on World Mission and Evangelism. Speaking on "The World in Which We Preach Christ," Mr. Thomas said:

   There is a growing sense of common humanity or human solidarity in the world which finds its expression in mutual concern, a sense of participation in the struggles of others for their fundamental rights, and a common endeavor in building structures of a world community and searching for an ethos to make them stable. This "secular ecumenical movement" may be only beginning, but it is already a genuine movement of human solidarity which we must recognize as a new factor of no small significance in the world today (In *Ecumenical Review*, April, 1964, pp. 261 f.).

   Soon thereafter the concept was brought to wider attention with an address in October, 1964, by A. H. van den Heuvel to the annual European Consultation of the WCC Youth Department in Zeist, Holland. This address on "The Secular Understanding of the Ecumenical" was published in the WCC journal *Youth* (November, 1964) and was later incorporated into Mr. van den Heuvel's book *The Humiliation of the Church* (London: SCM Press Ltd., 1966).

4. See volume 2 of this series, particularly the essay of Prof. C. Westermann.

5. R. McBrian, New York: Harper & Row, 1969.

6. R. Prenter, "Secularization as a Problem for Christian Dogmatics," *Lutheran World*, 1966, No. 4, p. 360.

7. "The Search for the Ecclesiological Quark," in *Lutheran World*, No. 1, 1970, p. 9: ". . . our reconceptualization of unity must involve seeing religious organization as systems rather than structures. . . . As a 'system,' the decisive criteria, the true 'marks' of its existence, are how it functions, acts, performs. The church too must be described by verbs rather than nouns. One of the basic cybernetic principles is that the structure of a machine or an organism is an 'index of the performance that may be expected from it'. . . ."

202 *Michael Rogness*

8. *The Church for Others,* Geneva, 1968, p. 16 f.
9. *Sources for Change,* ed. by H. T. Neve, Geneva, 1968, p. 59.
10. See for example the brief section "Roman Catholic Developments and the Church of the Future" in M. J. Heinecken's essay "The Scope of the Lordship of Christ" in *Christian Hope and the Lordship of Christ* (Ed. by M. J. Heinecken, Minneapolis: Augsburg Publishing House, 1969, pp. 85 f.). Consistent with its traditional "Aristotelian-Thomastic quantitatively progressive orientation," he writes, "Roman Catholicism now stresses this all-pervasive nature of God's presence: *Wherever, whenever, however,* life itself is furthered, instead of frustrated, stunted, perverted, plundered, there it is the Christ who is at work. . . . Every effort, therefore, which in some way contributes and furthers the life of man, the crown of creation, must be included in the scope of the Christ's gracious activity — whether this be the efforts of the revolutionaries giving their lives for their cause, scientists working long hours in the laboratory, or the United Nations meeting in arduous session, or whatever. It is all to be claimed for Christ" (p. 86).
11. See A. Röper's study *The Anonymous Christian,* New York: Sheed & Ward, 1966, and E. Schillebeeckx' "The Church and Mankind," in *Concilium,* vol. 1, No. 1, 1965.
12. *Lutheran World,* 1967, No. 1, p. 7.
13. "The Church in the Modern World," 38: The texts from Vatican II are quoted from *The Documents of Vatican II,* W. M. Abbott, S.J., ed., New York: Guild Press, 1966.
14. Reported by X. Rynne, *The Second Session,* London: Faber and Faber, 1963, p. 361 f.
15. *Unitas,* Summer, 1967, p. 108.
16. "The Church in the Modern World," 3.
17. *Introducing Contemporary Catholicism,* London: SCM Press, 1967, p. 38. Italics added.
18. *Righteousness and Society,* Philadelphia: Fortress Press, 1967, pp. 236, 239.
19. New York: Sheed and Ward, 1969, p. 6 f.
20. "Which Way for 'Faith and Order'? in *What Unity Implies,* World Council Study No. 7, Geneva, 1969, p. 119.
21. London: Burns & Oates, 1968.
22. "Toward a Wider Ecumenism," in *Ecumenical Theology,* No. 2, ed. by G. Baum, O.S.A., New York: Paulist Press, 1967, p. 70.
23. Para. 2.
24. *Augsburg Confession,* Article 7.
25. C. E. Braaten, "Ecumenism and Theological Education in the United States," in *Oecumenica 1969,* p. 204. Also *ibid.:*
    In a certain sense the seminary student today is a radical, so in love with Christ's mission to the world that in an odd way he hates the institutional church. He hates it to the extent that he is convinced that the church's institutional apparatus is an obstacle to ministry and servant-

hood. He is impatient and unwilling to wait for the professional ecclesiocrats to give him the green light for him to cooperate with anyone similarly interested in getting the job done. He has his own kind of ecumenism going for him, whose agenda is not made up of the doctrinal difficulties inherited from the past, but of the social problems sizzling in the present.

26. *Ecumenism*, 12.

27. "Ecumenism after Vatican Council II," in *Oecumenica 1967*, p. 157.

28. M. Goffin, "The Broken Pitcher: An Essay on the Present Christian Crisis," in *The Future of Catholic Christianity*, ed. by M. de la Bedoyere, London: Constable & Company, 1966, p. 66.
Also *ibid:*

> From now on it will become more and more plain that however much accustomed allegiances may influence our thinking, the old confessional differences are anachronistic and fundamentally irrelevant. The lines of demarcation lie not between this or that church, but between groups of people from any denomination who offer different solutions to those problems common to all.

29. See R. Campbell, O.P., *Spectrum of Catholic Attitudes*.

30. T. Early, "A New Challenge to the Ecumenical Movement," in *The Lamp*, September, 1969, p. 14.

31. Newbigin, *ibid.*, p. 117.

32. *Ecumenism*, 12: The Council also specified that such joint cooperation was not just a matter of single Christians working together, but that the corporate church should engage itself actively. *The Church's Missionary Activity*, 15.
The late Augustin Cardinal Bea, the leading inspiration behind the Council's *Decree on Ecumenism*, wrote of those matters on which doctrinally divided Christians can cooperate:

> Christians certainly can, even without unity in faith, coordinate their efforts in defence of the general Christian cause and of religious liberty, in works of charity, and in many social areas. For instance, in some countries Christians have taken the initiative in forming a banking institution to lend money at low rates of interest to young married couples *(Unity in Freedom*, New York: Harper & Row, 1964, p. 188).

33. The work of R. Shaull at Princeton Theological Seminary illustrates this direction. He is Professor of Ecumenics, a chair one would expect would devote itself to such matters as the historical factors causing church division, the history of ecumenism, the changing state of doctrinal diversity, and so on. Yet Mr. Shaull has become known for his lectures and publications on social ethics, particularly for his opinions regarding the church's role in revolutionary situations. Many are, in fact, surprised upon discovering that he is actually a professor of ecumenics, but the social and human concern of his work is precisely that which secular ecumenism foresees as the true focus of ecumenism.

34. "More than Church Unity," in *Lutheran World*, No. 1, 1970, pp. 43 f.

35. Newbigin, *ibid.*, p. 128 f.

36. In 1969 the Faith and Order Commission published an extremely helpful

study document on "The Unity of the Church and the Unity of Mankind" (In *Study Encounter*, No. 4, 1969, p. 163 f.). In attempting to clarify and elucidate the problem in its ecumenical context, the authors note that "this theme today occupies the center of the stage" and warn: "The concept of the unity of mankind is not to be treated as a slogan, still less as a magic formula" (p. 163 f.). The first section of the document deals with biblical considerations and concludes that "it becomes increasingly clear that God's action embraces all mankind" and "when the Gospel speaks of reconciliation, peace and unity it does so on the assumption that in Jesus Christ men really become one" (p. 167). In reflecting upon the systematic aspects of the question, the authors reiterate: "The central theological problem raised by this consideration concerns the role of Christ" (p. 171). In the following sections of "Ecclesiological Considerations" and "The Unity of the Church" an attempt is made to list the questions which arise in relating the unity of man to the unity of the church.

Realizing the magnitude of the topic, the authors entitle the last paragraph "The Staggering Size of the Task" and conclude with this statement: "If the church is to be an active factor on the way to the unity of mankind, vast changes in understanding, in ethics, and in structures are needed so that the divisive factors may be discarded as restricting husks" (p. 178).

AUTHORS

Günther Gassmann, Germany, Th.D., research professor, Institute for Ecumenical Research in Strasbourg, France.

Leonhard Goppelt, Germany, D.Dr. Professor of New Testament, Faculty of Protestant Theology in Munich, Germany

Marc Lienhard, France, Th.D., assistant research professor, Institute for Ecumenical Research in Strasbourg, France

Harding Meyer, Germany, Th.D., research professor, Institute for Ecumenical Research in Strasbourg, France

Warren A. Quanbeck, USA, Th.D., professor of systematic theology, Luther Theological Seminary in St. Paul, Minnesota

Michael Rogness, USA, Th.D., pastor at First Lutheran Church, Duluth, Minn., formerly assistant research professor, Institute for Ecumenical Research in Strasbourg, France

Gérard Siegwalt, France, Th.D., professor of systematic theology at the Protestant Theological Faculty in Strasbourg, France

Vilmos Vajta, Sweden, Th.D., D.D., research professor, Institute for Ecumenical Research in Strasbourg, France